Kodak

Pocket Guide to Photographing Your Cat

Simon and Schuster/New York

Published by Simon and Schuster
A Division of Simon and Schuster, Inc.
Simon and Schuster Building
Rockefeller Center
1230 Avenue of the Americas
New York, New York 10020

SIMON and SCHUSTER and Colophon are registered trademarks of Simon and Schuster

Library of Congress Cataloging in Publication Data
Main entry under title:

KODAK Pocket Guide to Photographing Your Cat

Includes index.
1. Photography of cats. I. Eastman Kodak Company
TR729.C3K63 1985 778-9'32 85-2405
ISBN 0-671-50671-4

Manufactured in the United States of America

1 2 3 4 5 6 7 8 9 10

Written for Kodak by Robert Adkinson Limited
Editors: Susan Victor (S&S), Richard Platt (RAL)
Editorial coordination: Derek Doeffinger (Kodak)
Kenneth Oberg (Kodak)
Jacalyn Salitan (Kodak)
Design: Roy Williams (RAL)
Production: Charles Styles (Kodak)
Howard M. Goldstein (S&S)
Photo Credits: All photos by Paddy Cutts, except the following: ARDEA 71, 72, 85; Richard Platt 53 bottom, 56, 57 top; Sally Ann Thompson 55, 73 top, 82 top, 99 top, 101 center.
Illustrations: Rick Blakeley

The Kodak materials described in this publication for use with cameras are available from those dealers normally supplying Kodak products. Other materials may be used, but equivalent results may not be obtained.

CONTENTS

INTRODUCTION

Cats are among the camera's most appealing subjects. Their visual attraction is obvious: whose heart doesn't soften at the sight of a little kitten nestling in the palm of a hand? But there is more to a cat's appeal than appearance alone. Every cat is a unique character, with quirks, habits and foibles all of its own. Capture a cat's individuality on film, and you'll have a fine picture that is as full of interest and charm as any human portrait.

Sometimes taking such pictures is easy: cats will often sit and pose proudly for a portrait. But when it suits them, they can be haughty and aloof, strutting independently and disdainfully flicking their tails at the camera.

This book gives you the how-to basics to photograph even the most arrogant cat. Packed in this pocket-size volume you'll find not only facts and advice about photography, but also useful tips that will ensure that you get more cooperation from your cat—at moments which you choose, rather than just when the cat decides it's time for a picture. So whether your camera is snapshot-simple, or super-sophisticated, there's plenty in this book for you.

To begin, let's take a look at how other photographers picture their cats. Turn the page, and you'll seen an album of exciting cat pictures that will give you lots of ideas and inspiration. Go to it with your cat and your camera, and you'll soon be taking photos every bit as good as these.

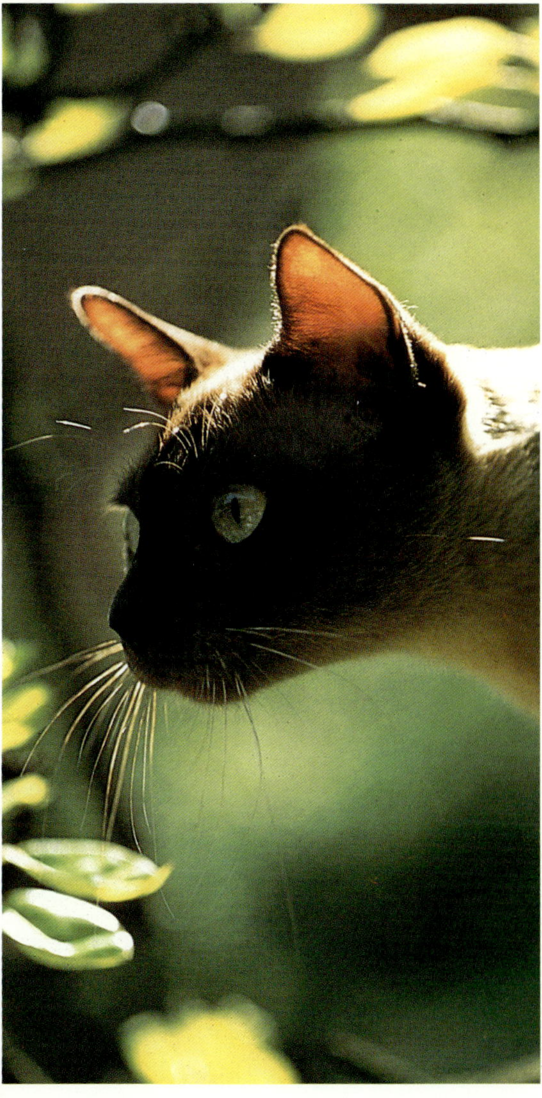

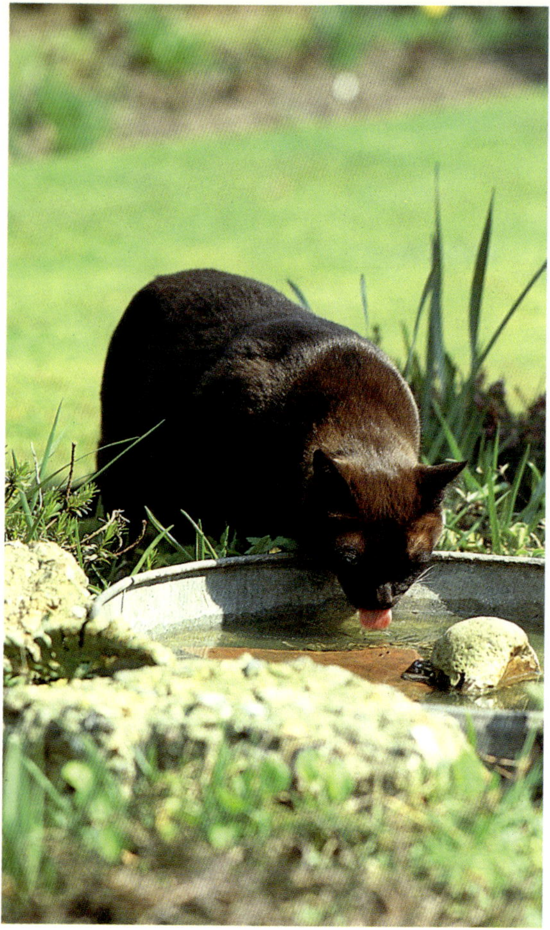

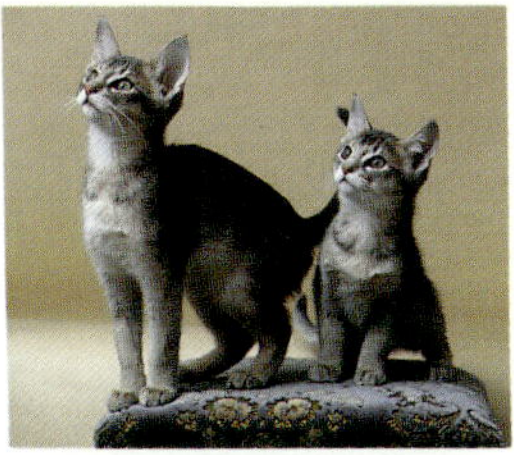

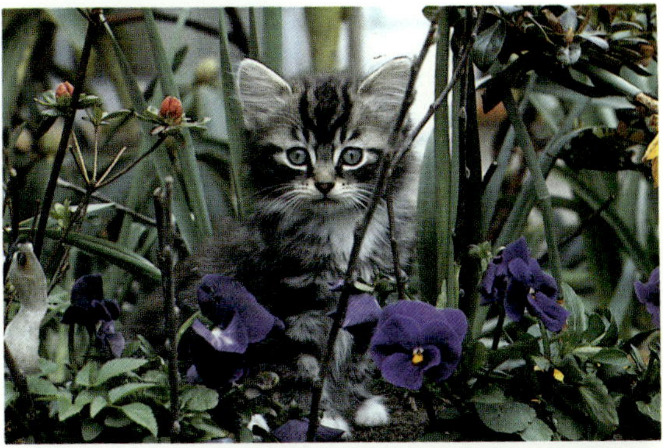

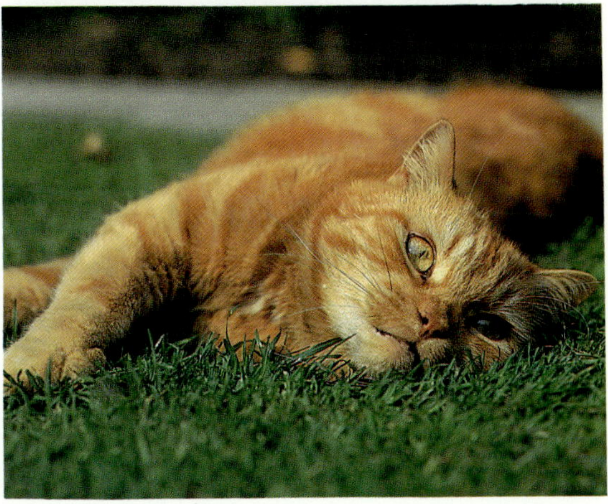

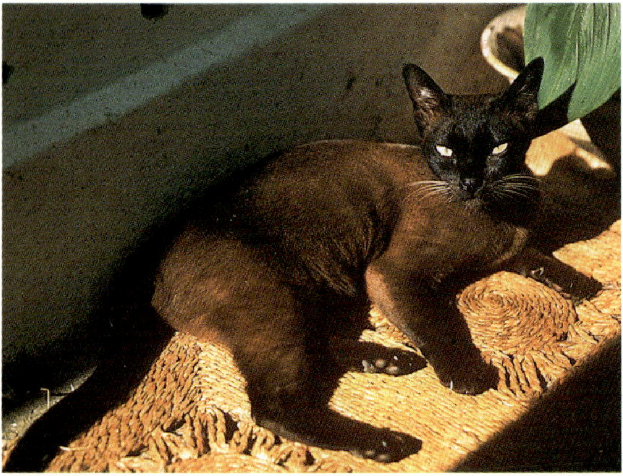

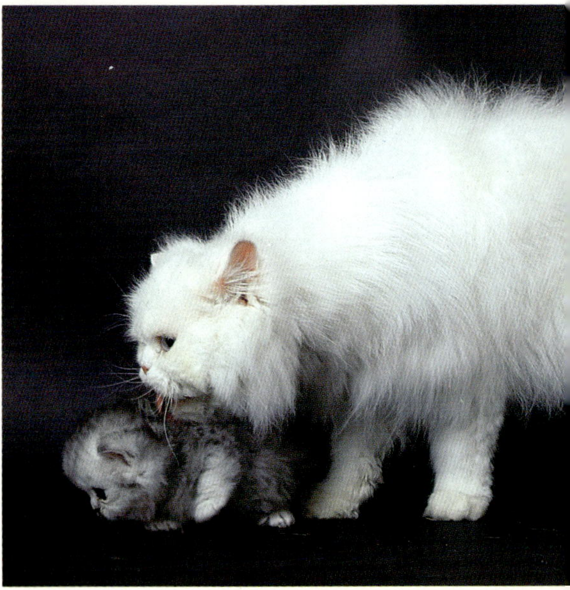

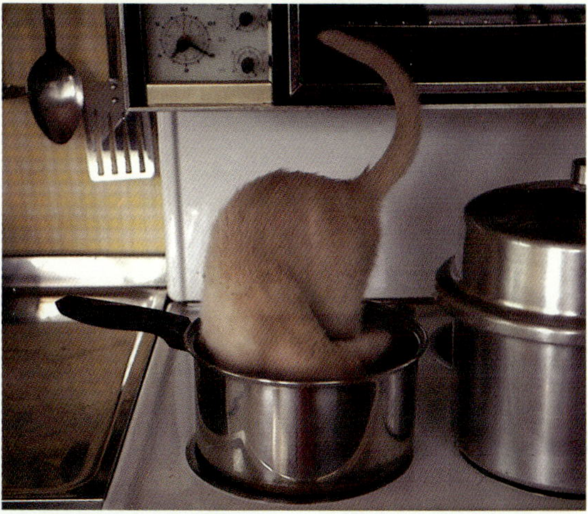

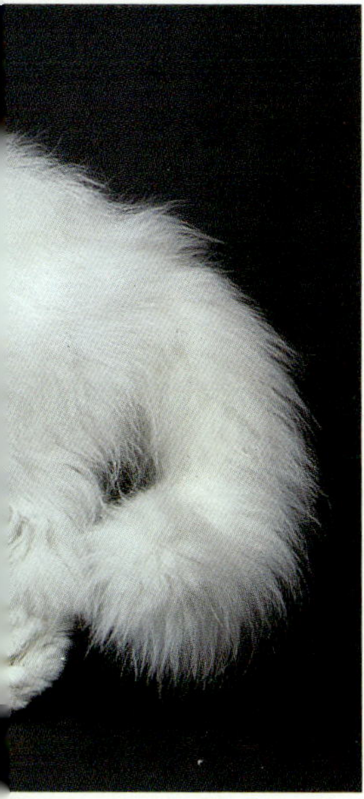

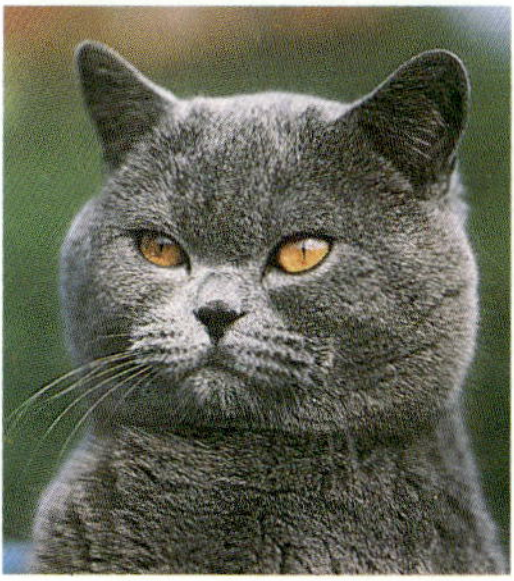

GETTING STARTED

You can use any type of camera to take good pictures of cats. After all, the camera is only a tool in the hands of the photographer, and as the old saying goes, only a bad worker blames the tools. With even simple cameras, enthusiastic photographers can coax wonderful pictures from their pets; but the most sophisticated modern camera will never make up for a photographer's impatience or a lack of sympathy for the cat in front of the lens.

Whether you are using a simple snapshot camera or a sophisticated SLR, you'll get more out of it if you know something about how your camera works. A little understanding of the limitations of the equipment you're using will save you many hours of frustration and rolls of wasted film. Equally, before you consider buying complex and expensive equipment it's worth knowing whether you're fully exploiting the potential of your current camera.

The section that follows explains the differences beteen popular types of cameras; it goes on to take a close look at the features and controls that are of particular importance when cats are the subject of the picture. Here you'll find hints and tips that will help you make the most of any camera, and simple photographic techniques which you can use to get better, more characteristic pictures of your cat.

Careful Composition

Most simple cameras don't make sharp pictures when the cat is closer than 3 or 4 ft.(1 m), but this needn't limit your photography. Here the photographer's elegant, considered composition more than makes up for the cat's small size in the frame.

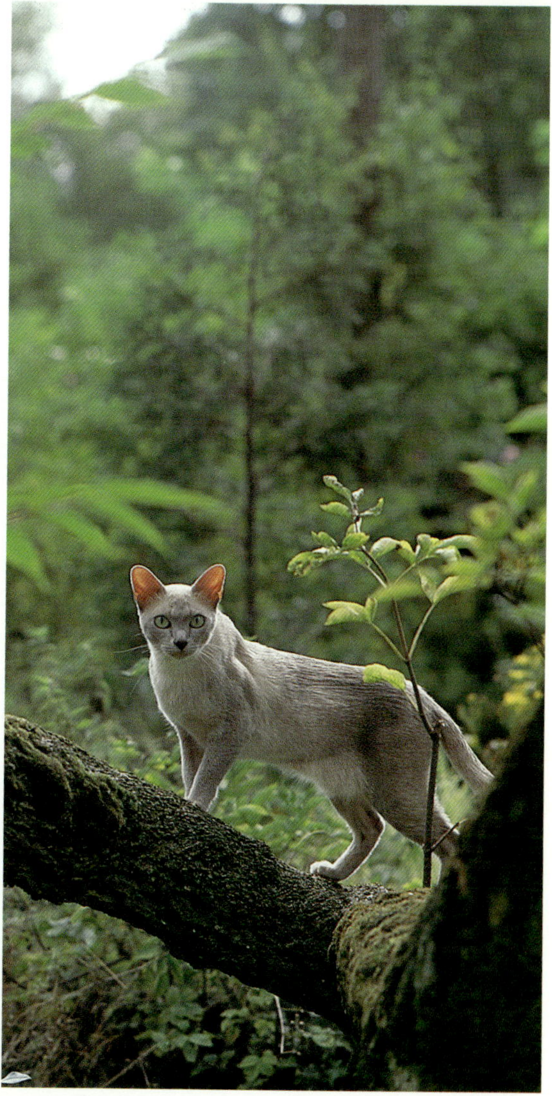

CATS AND CAMERAS

The best camera for photographing your cat is the one in your pocket, or one that you can grab at a moment's notice. Cats are independent-minded creatures, and they invariably resist any persuasion to repeat their most charming antics. Only by keeping your camera handy and ready can you be sure to catch your cat at its best moments.

This is where simple and automatic cameras really score. You can keep a loaded disc, 110 or 35 mm compact camera constantly at the ready: on a shelf in the home, or in your pocket if you're out in the yard with the cat. Since these models need little or no adjustment, you can be taking pictures almost as soon as the camera's at your eye, so you need never miss the twitch of a whisker.

35 mm single-lens-reflex (SLR) cameras are bulkier and heavier, but many of the newer ones are as automated as their smaller cousins. Their principal advantages are the control they offer the photographer over the way the cat appears on film, and the tremendous range of accessories with which they can be fitted. An SLR is really the heart of a whole photographic system, and if you can afford it, this is probably the ideal camera for photographing cats.

Cameras larger than the 35 mm format offer few advantages, unless you intend to make very big prints of your pet, or submit your pictures for publication in magazines and books.

Cat in Close-Up
Cameras with close-focus settings let you get this close to your cat.

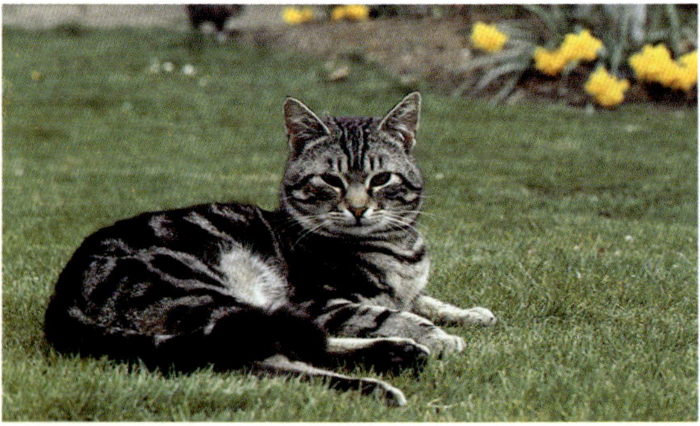

Disc Cameras

Disc cameras are inexpensive, and easy to load and use. Their slim profile means they won't bulge your pocket. If buying a disc camera for cat photography, choose a model with a slide-in close-focusing lens, such as the KODAK Disc 6100 Camera. The close-focusing feature enables you to fill the picture area with a cat portrait.

KODAK Disc Cameras have automatic exposure, automatic film advance, and a built-in flash unit that turns itself on and off. The automatic film advance lets you take several pictures of your cat in action without winding film manually between frames. And the flash stops action indoors, enabling you to take sharp pictures of your pet pouncing dramatically on a ball of wool, or some imagined prey.

110 and 126 Cameras

These cameras are also light weight and compact. Film loading is equally easy—a cartridge (rather than a flat disc) just drops into the back of the camera. Exposure setting is usually automatic so there are no controls to adjust. Many, such as the KODAK EKTRALITE 10 Camera have a built-in flash, but only a few have motorized film advance. Generally, though, cartridge-loading cameras are not as sophisticated as disc cameras, and cannot make sharp pictures of subjects closer than about five feet, so you won't be able to get close enough to fill the frame with your cat. This is not an insurmountable problem; you may be able to buy accessories which let you move closer; and you can always get bigger prints made, then trim them down to remove the unwanted details around the cat.

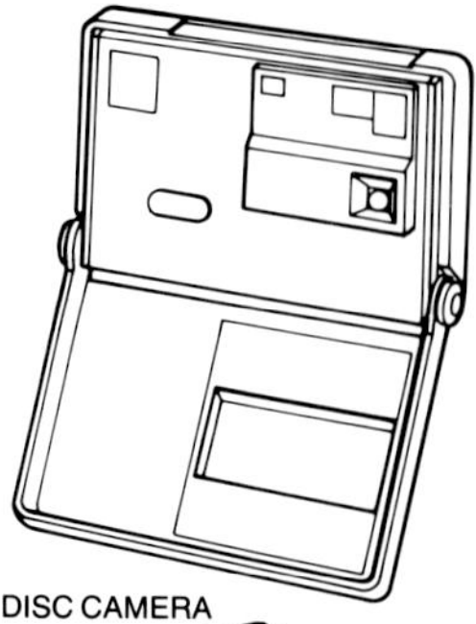

DISC CAMERA

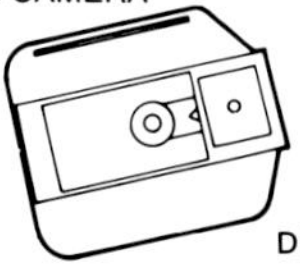

DISC FILM

110 CAMERA

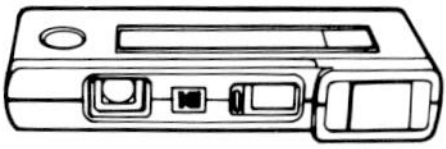

110 FILM CARTRIDGE

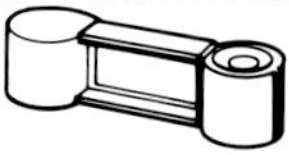

126 CAMERA

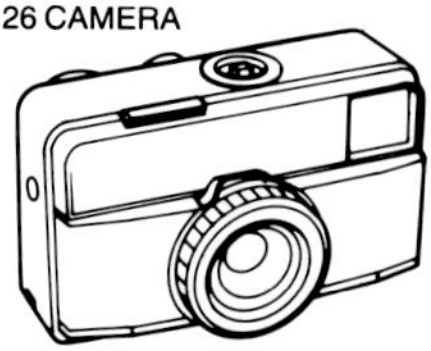

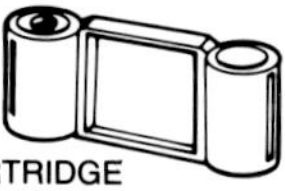

126 FILM CARTRIDGE

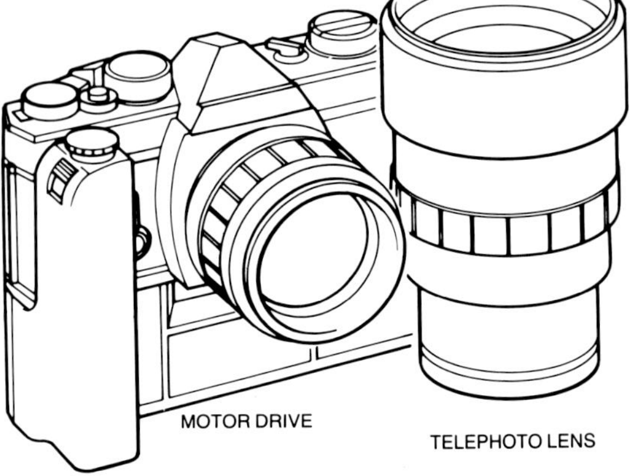

35 mm Single-Lens-Reflex Cameras (SLRs)

These are possibly the most adaptable and useful cameras available, and certainly the best for cat photography. An SLR has the great advantage that a single lens is used for both viewing the subject and taking the picture. What you see in the viewfinder is therefore exactly what appears on film and framing or focusing is easy and precise. Simpler types of camera have separate viewing and taking lenses, and this can lead to errors in composition in close-ups: the cat's tail may appear in the viewfinder, but not in the photograph.

All SLRs have interchangeable lenses: you can swap the lens supplied with the camera for a telephoto lens, which has a narrower field of view. With one of these lenses on the camera you can frame a tightly cropped portrait of your cat without getting so close as to startle it. SLRs can also be fitted with wide-angle lenses, which take in a broader field of view, but these are of little value with subjects as small as a cat.

With any SLR, you can move quite close to the cat, and still keep it sharp in the picture. The limit is usually about 18 in (0.4 m). And with inexpensive accessories, you can move even closer, perhaps filling the frame with a whisker-to-whisker view.

Almost all SLRs are at least partially automatic, which is useful if you want to take quick-fire action photos. If you are buying a new camera, though, get one that also gives you the option of manual control. You'll find this facility useful for taking out-of-the-ordinary pictures of your cat, or in unusual lighting conditions.

35 mm Compact Cameras

SLR cameras are neither light nor inexpensive—and not everyone needs the versatility that they offer. "Compact" and auto-focus 35 mm cameras use the same large-size film as SLRs, yet they are almost as small and easy to use as 110 and disc cameras. They often share the same features, too, such as automatic film advance and built-in flash and may provide auto-focusing.

Unfortunately, though, convenience is not all they inherit from the smaller cameras that they sometimes resemble. They also have the same limitations on subject distance—so you may not be able to get a sharp picture when your cat is closer than about three or four feet.

INSTANT CAMERA

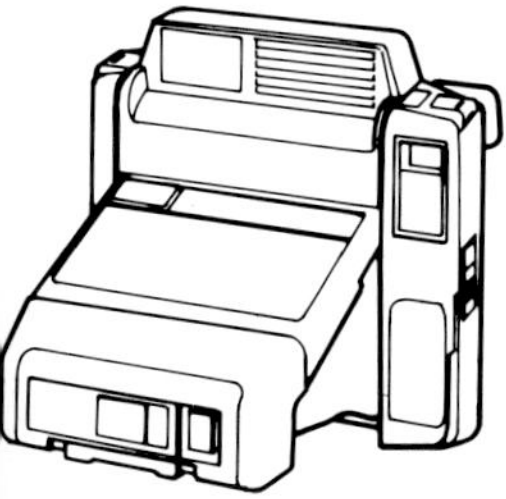

Instant-Picture Cameras ▲

These cameras are bigger than the other snapshot cameras, but have the advantage of giving a finished print minutes after you take the picture. They, too, usually have automatic exposure and built-in flash. Some are fixed focus while others are auto-focus—either way, they take care of the focusing.

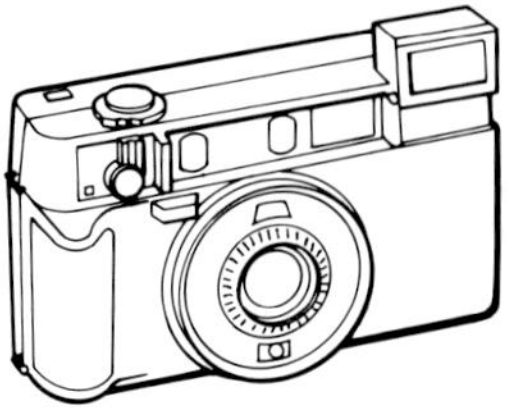

35 mm COMPACT AUTOFOCUS CAMERA

35 mm Film

Both SLR and compact cameras use 35 mm film, which is supplied in metal magazines. Though a little more difficult to load than disc or cartridge film, 35 mm has two big advantages. First, there are more film types available, whereas with a disc camera, for example, you can only make color prints—not black-and-white, or slides for projection.

The other advantage is the film's large size. Pictures taken using a 35 mm camera need very much less enlargement than disc or 110 and are sharper and much clearer as a result.

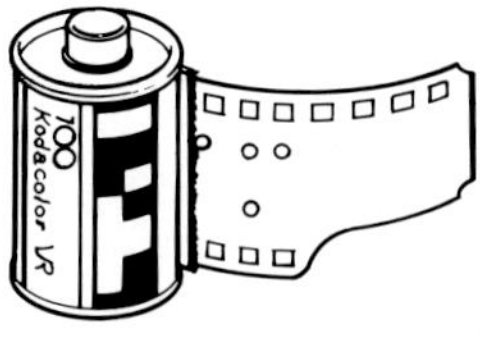

CONTROLLING SHARPNESS

A camera can make sharp pictures only within a limited range of subject distances. Sometimes this range is very broad: many 110 cameras, for example, will keep cats sharp as long as camera and subject are at least 4 or 5 feet apart. With adjustable cameras, there is more control over sharpness. They not only allow you to choose the precise distance at which subjects are sharp, but also let you decide whether things at greater and lesser distances will be clear or blurred in the picture. For example, on such an adjustable camera, you could choose to keep the cat near the camera sharp, yet turn an ugly background to a featureless blur.

If you have a fixed-focus or auto-focus camera, making sharp pictures of your cat just means ensuring that you don't get too close. On other cameras you'll need to focus manually, either by estimating how far you are from the cat and setting this on a distance scale; or with an SLR, by turning a ring on the lens, until the cat actually looks sharp and clear in the viewfinder. This technique is the most accurate of all.

Focusing an SLR Camera

The lens of an SLR projects an image of the subject via a mirror up to a matte screen. When you press the shutter release, the mirror flips up, and the image goes instead to the film. Thus the image you see on the screen is identical to the image on film, and when one is sharp, both will be sharp.

Molded into the middle of the screen are focusing aids—regular patterns which help you to focus. Most split unsharp subjects, either into halves, or into a regular geometric pattern. Turning the focusing ring unites the halves, or erases the "shattered" appearance.

Auto-focus Cameras

With one of these cameras you will have few problems keeping the subject sharp—as long as it is central in the viewfinder. Off-center subjects will confuse the distance-measurement system, so that the camera focuses on an irrelevant feature. You can overcome this difficulty if the camera has a focus-lock control which allows you to preset the focus and then recompose the picture, before pressing the shutter release. Details vary so consult the camera's instructions.

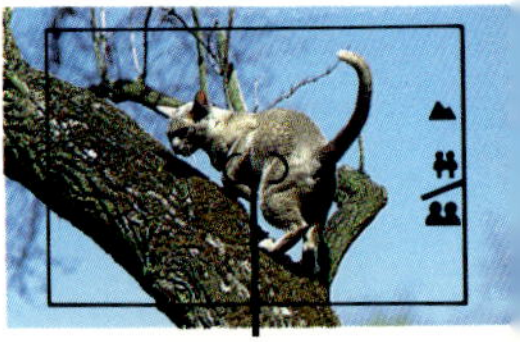

DISTANCE MEASURING AREA

How Much Will Be Sharp?

Once you have focused the camera, how do you know how much of the scene will be sharp on film, and how do you control how far on either side of the subject the zone of sharp focus extends?

The extent of this zone is called the depth of field, and is controlled by the camera's aperture. This is literally an aperture—a hole of variable size within the lens itself. The larger the hole, the less of the picture will be sharp; small apertures keep more in focus, as shown below.

On most cameras that have an adjustable aperture, its size is changed by a control ring around the lens. The size of the aperture is referred to in terms of *f*-stops: numbers which are engraved on the aperture control ring. The larger the number, the smaller is the size of the aperture; *f*/16 is a small aperture, and *f*/2.8 large.

Controlling the size of the aperture has another affect, besides changing depth of field. Large apertures let through more light, and this affects exposure, as explained on page 20.

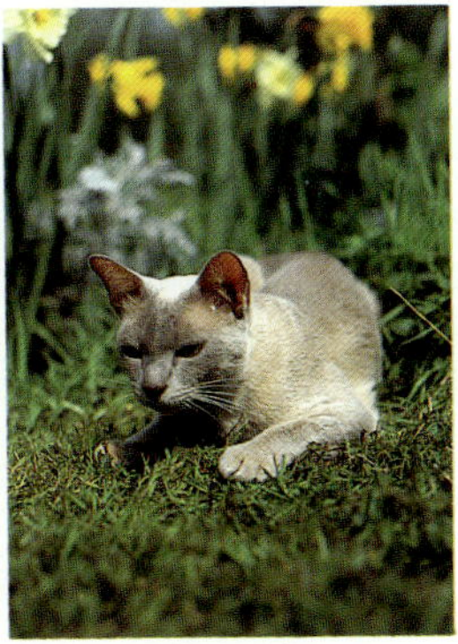

f/2.8 ONLY CAT SHARP

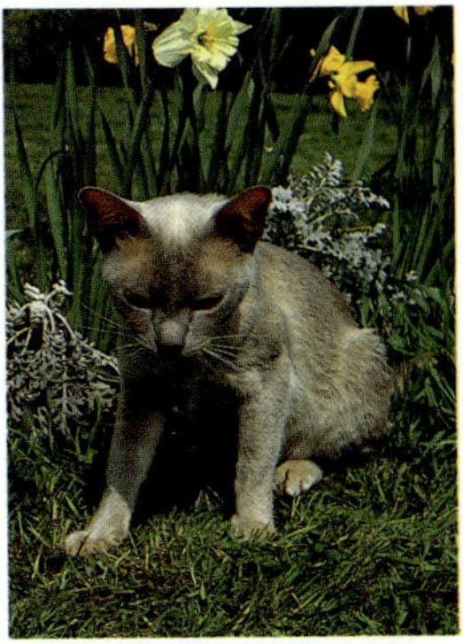

f/16 MOST OF PICTURE SHARP

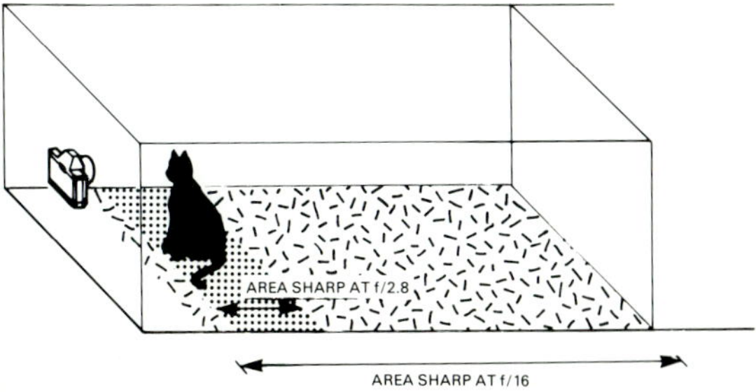

CONTROLLING MOVEMENT

Cats are active, busy creatures; they prowl around, spring at leaves blowing in the wind, and scamper along roofs and walls. Even when fast asleep they often twitch their tails and legs in pursuit of a dreamed-up adversary.

How the cat's movements are represented in your pictures depends on the shutter. This is a device which operates like a blind, opening to let the image of the subject reach the film for a short time, then snapping shut again to keep unwanted light out of the camera. If the shutter opens for just a brief time—a fast shutter speed—the cat's actions will appear arrested in mid-flow. A slow shutter speed will blur the cat's movements into soft, flowing lines.

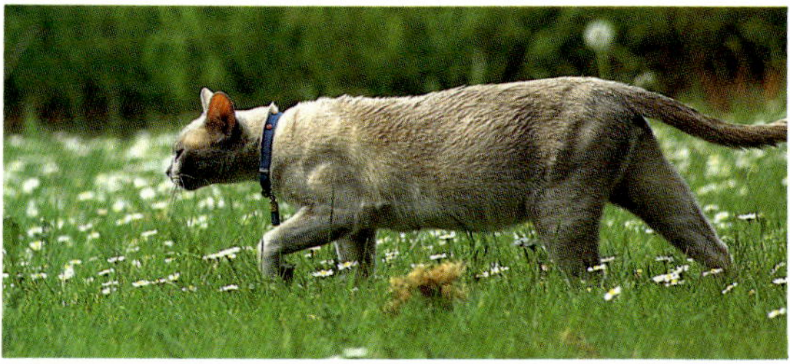

Cat's Pause

Simple cameras make clear pictures only of slow-moving cats.

Setting the Shutter Speed

How the shutter speed is set depends on the type of camera. The simplest cameras, though, give you no choice, because they have just one shutter speed: their shutters open for about a one-hundredth of a second (usually written just as 1/100) every time you take a picture. This is fast enough to arrest the small movements of a cat when it is sitting down, but not when walking or jumping. So if you have a simple snapshot camera, photograph moving cats only when you are deliberately aiming for a blurred effect.

All other cameras have a range of shutter speeds, but these are not always under the photographer's control. For example, with compact 35 mm and disc models, the camera itself automatically chooses the speed that will give correct exposure for the lighting conditions. Bright light causes the camera to set a fast shutter speed; dim light, a slow one.

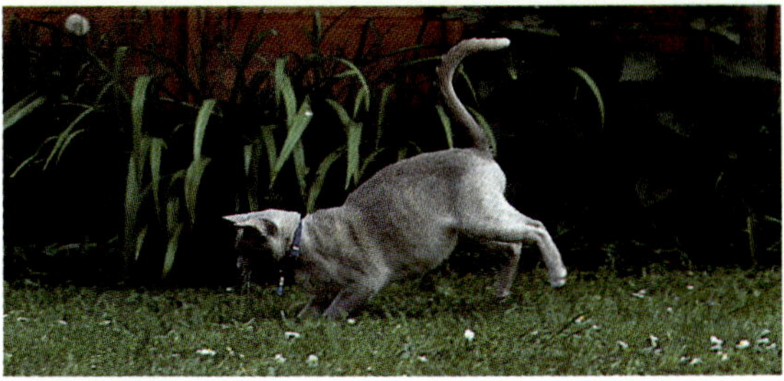

A Flying Leap
Freezing this cat's movements demanded a fast shutter speed—1/1000.

Most SLR cameras allow you to choose the shutter speed, and thereby control how a moving cat appears on film.

The method of adjusting the shutter speed depends on the camera you have, and how automatic it is. Usually there is a dial marked with speeds, start at 1 (for one second) and running 2 (½ second), 4, 8, and so on, to 1000 (1/1000). However, your camera may have buttons which when pressed change a digital display of speed in the camera's viewfinder.

Control over shutter speed may even be indirect. If you have an aperture-preferred automatic camera, you may be able to alter shutter speed only by changing the camera's aperture. The automatic meter will then respond by altering the speed, which you can monitor by watching a display in the viewfinder.

Holding the Camera Still
Just as a cat's motion blurs its image in pictures taken at a slow shutter speed, so too movements of the camera can blur the whole picture. This effect is called camera shake, and usually ruins pictures—whereas subject blurring can actually make quite an evocative, moody image of your cat.

You can eliminate camera shake when handholding your camera with its normal lens by setting a speed faster than 1/60. If the camera is locked onto a tripod, you can set slower speeds and still get sharp pictures of static objects, but remember that a shutter speed of 1/30 second or slower is sure to blur even slow movements of a cat.

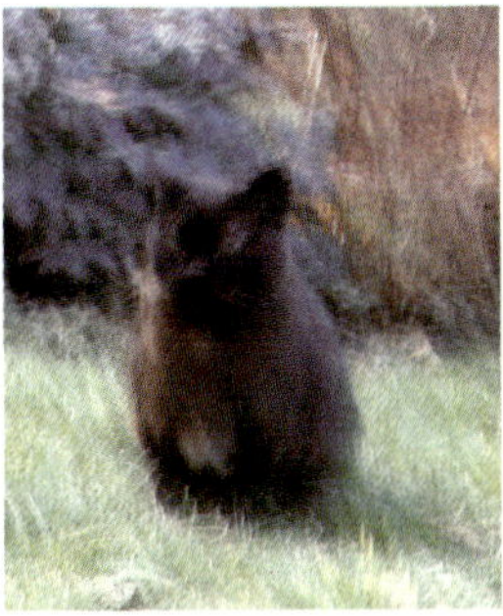

CONTROLLING EXPOSURE

To make a good picture, film must get just the right amount of light—what photographers call "correct exposure". Too much light, or overexposure, makes a picture in which the bright parts of the subject are burned out to white. Too little light produces underexposure, and your prints will come out with dull, muddy colors.

Usually the camera itself takes care of all exposure settings. If you have an SLR, though, you can intervene and adjust the controls yourself, in order to deliberately set an extreme value—perhaps using the fastest shutter speed available to arrest all movement.

Light and Film

Before your camera chooses how to set the shutter speed and aperture, it needs to know how sensitive the film is to light, and how much light the subject is reflecting. The film's sensitivity, or speed, is printed as an ISO value on the box and magazine. With most 35 mm cameras you must transfer this setting onto the camera's film speed dial as shown on page 24. Light-sensitive cells inside the camera measure the light reflected from the subject. The camera then indicates in the viewfinder the aperture and shutter speed for correct exposure and, if a fully automatic camera, will set them.

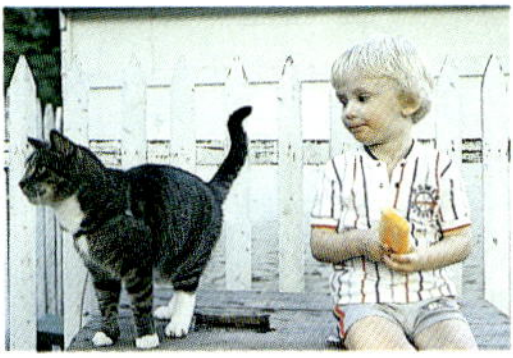

OVEREXPOSED

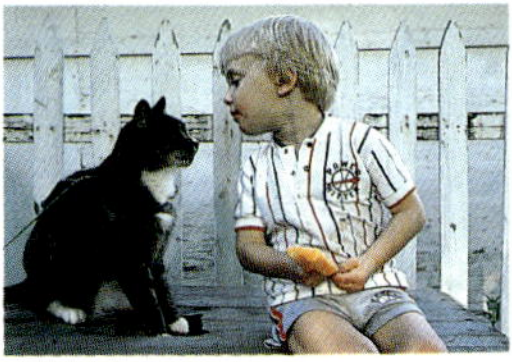

CORRECTLY EXPOSED

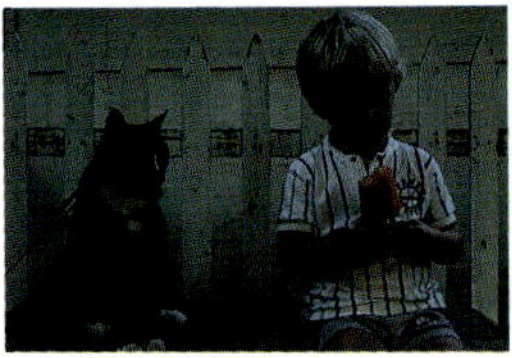

UNDEREXPOSED

If you decide to control the exposure manually, you can use either shutter speed or aperture to alter the exposure, because both controls affect the overall amount of light that gets to the film. The aperture adjusts **how bright** is the light that reaches the film, and the shutter speed controls **how long** the exposure lasts. If you halve the shutter speed, and double the size of the aperture, the overall level of exposure is unchanged, so for each particular light level and film speed there is a wide choice of possible shutter speeds and apertures.

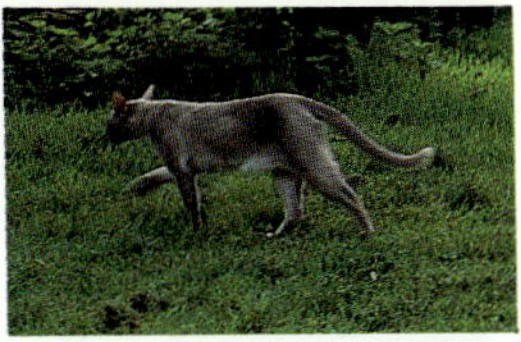

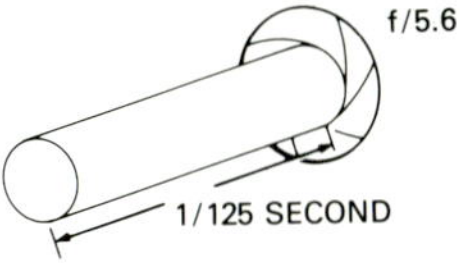

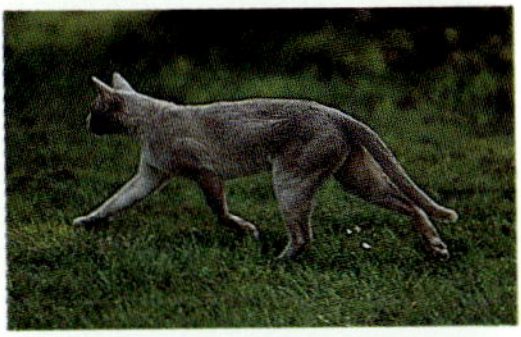

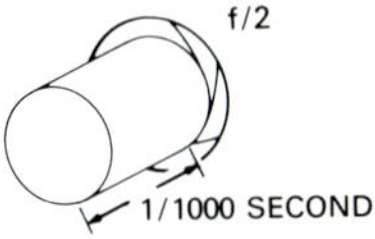

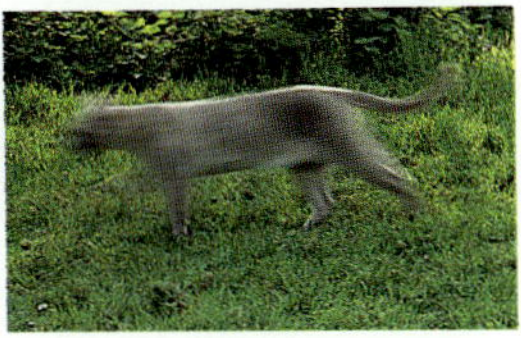

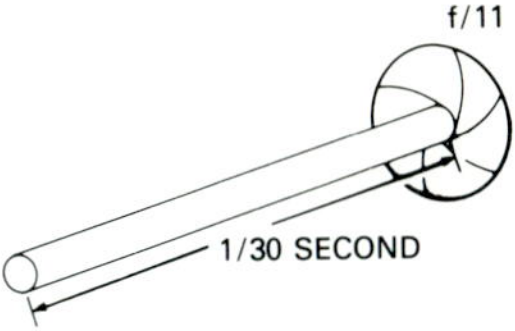

Action or Depth?
An automatic camera sets the exposure to 1/125 at *f*/5.6 for this scene (top). But the photographer could equally have chosen 1/1000 at *f*/2 to stop the running cat's movement (center), or 1/30 at *f*/11 to keep the background sharp (bottom). All would have yielded the correct level of exposure.

Non-Average Subjects

Your camera's meter is designed to work best with average subjects—that's to say, subjects that have dark and light areas in about equal amounts. With subjects that are predominatly dark, or mainly light in tone, the meter may occasionally give incorrect exposure.

You are unlikely to notice this exposure inaccuracy except when you make close-up pictures of light-furred cats. At these times, give extra exposure by setting your camera's exposure compensation dial to +1 or ×2. If your camera is not fitted with such a control, set the ISO dial to half the speed of the film in use—but don't forget to set it back again after taking the picture.

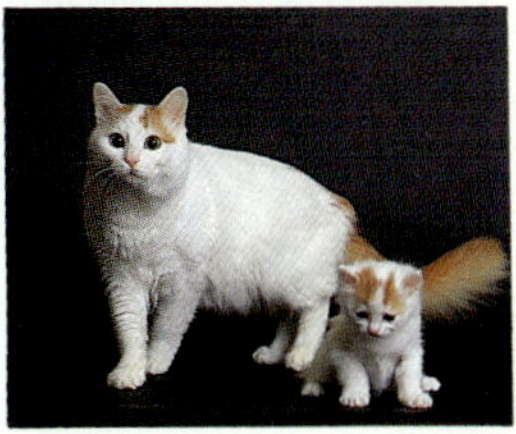

HOW TO GET CLOSER

Cats are pretty small: rarely longer than about a foot and a half, plus tail. If you have an SLR camera you can buy one of a number of accessories to get closer, as explained at right, and a few of these are also available for less complex cameras. And some disc and 110 cameras have either a close-up setting or a telephoto control. Both of these features move a small lens into place behind the camera's main lens. The first shifts the camera's focusing range—usually to bring into focus subjects between about 2 feet and 4 feet (0.6—1.3 m) distant. A telephoto setting, on the other hand, does not allow you to get physically closer. Instead it enlarges the center of the picture, so that your cat almost fills the frame at the camera's normal minimum focusing distance.

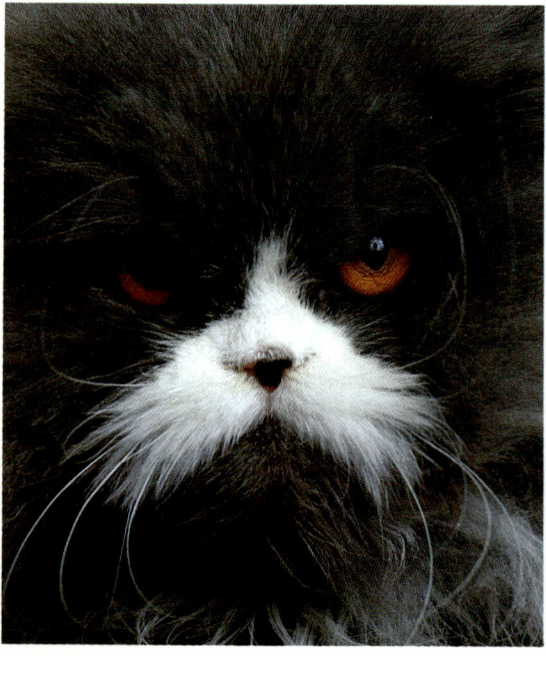

Close-up Attachments

The simplest and most inexpensive of these is the supplementary close-up lens which fits in front of any lens that has a screw thread around it. The most useful type is a "+1", or "one diopter" lens—with this fitted, you can usually make sharp pictures when your cat is between 20 inches and 3 feet (0.5—1 m) away, or less with an SLR.

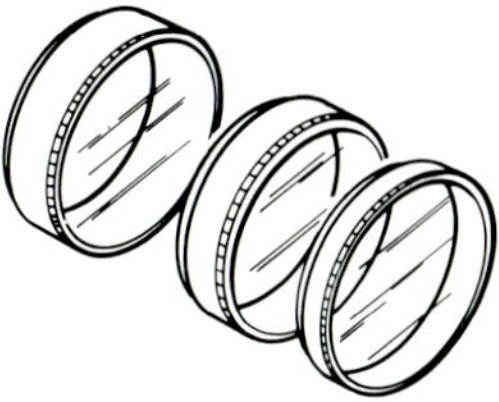

SUPPLEMENTARY CLOSE-UP LENSES

For SLRs, you can buy extension tubes, which fit between the lens and camera body. Sold in sets of three, these are not cheap, but allow you to get close enough to fill the frame with the cat's eye if you want to! They are slightly more difficult to use than close-up lenses, and require some compensation to exposure when you use flash.

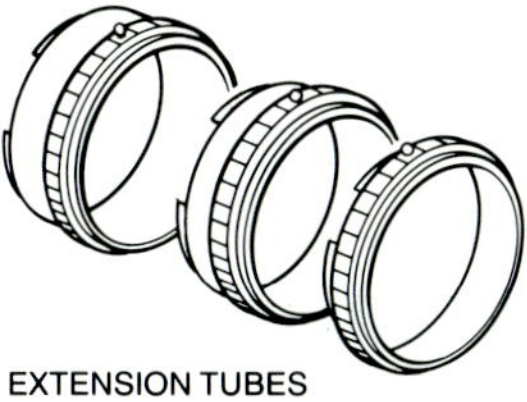

EXTENSION TUBES

A macro lens makes close-up pictures with an SLR very simple. It takes the place of a standard lens, but focuses continuously from the distance down to about 10 inches (0.25 m). These lenses, though, are costly—perhaps half as expensive as your camera.

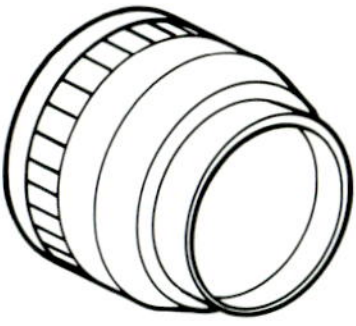

MACRO LENS

Close-up Framing

Most non-SLR cameras have marks in the viewfinder that show how much of a **distant** subject will be recorded on film. In addition to the main frame-lines, though, you'll usually see a couple of small marks, as shown at right. These marks indicate the field of view for nearby subjects. Always keep the cat inside these marks when making close-ups, or its tail or feet will be cropped out of the picture on film.

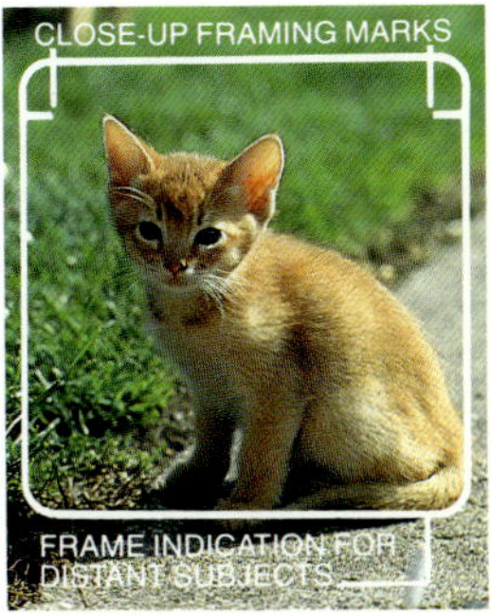

PICKING THE BEST FILM

Films come in three basic forms: color negative film for making color prints; color transparency film, which makes slides for projection; and black-and-white negative film, which produces monochrome prints. The choice between black-and-white and color is purely personal, but should you use negative film or transparencies and what speed film should you use?

These two film types each have their own technical advantages and drawbacks, as outlined at right. However, your choice will probably be influenced less by these technical considerations than by the way you plan to show your pictures. Prints are easy to hand around or carry in a wallet, but slides, on the other hand, need to be magnified with a viewer or projector. Though this seems inconvenient, a slide blown up to mural-size on a screen has an impact no postcard-size print can match.

Film Speed

Not all films have equal sensitivity to light. "Fast" films are very sensitive to light and have a high ISO number. KODACOLOR VR 400 and VR 1000 Films are fast films. Slow films such as KODACHROME 25 Film have low ISO numbers indicating their very much lower sensitivity. You'll find the ISO number printed on the film pack, and usually the film's name also includes the speed.

Film speed is important in everyday photography because it affects exposure. A slow film needs more exposure—which means a slower shutter speed or a wider aperture. To get a fast shutter speed with a slow film you'd have to take the picture in bright light.

Fast film gives you more versatility, because it enables you to take pictures of your cat in dimmer light, and to use smaller apertures or faster shutter speeds in bright light. There is a catch, though: the faster the film, the more visible is its gritty image structure, or grain. With 35 mm films of ISO 400 or slower, you are unlikely to notice the grain on enlargements of even up to 8 × 10 inches.

Because they're smaller, 110 films need more enlargement than 35 mm, and grain in enlargements may be quite noticeable when you use a fast film.

FILM SPEED SCALE

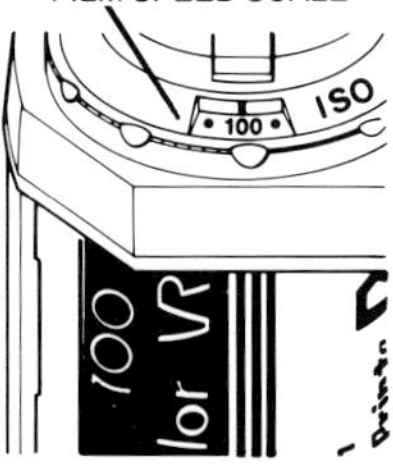

Setting Film Speed
Transfer the ISO number printed on the film magazine to the camera's film speed dial.

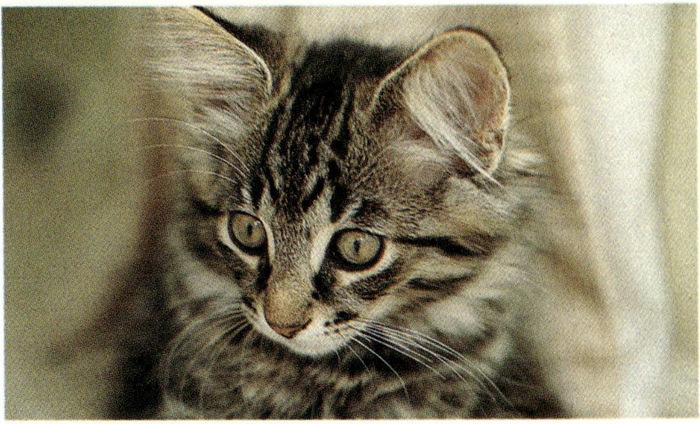

Color Negative Film ▲
This type of film is tolerant of exposure errors, and gives its best results in daylight or with flash. It will also give acceptable results in regular electric light without the bother of filters. It's easy and cheap to get extra prints made from negatives, too.

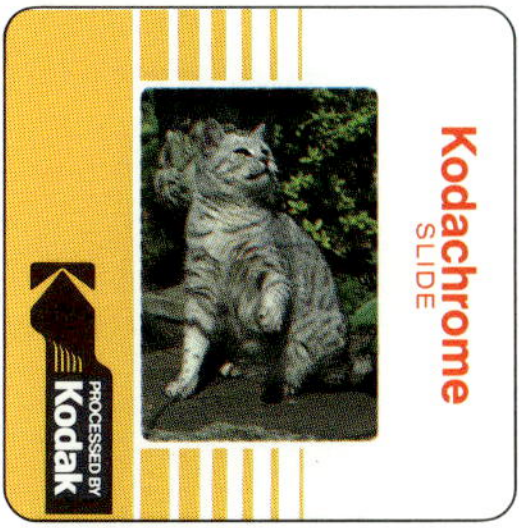

Color Slides ▶
These look great when projected on a screen or white wall, but the film needs careful exposure for good results. If you take color slides indoors by ordinary room lights, you must either use special filters over the lens to get the colors right, or use special tungsten-balanced film. Prints can be made from slides, but are more costly than prints from negatives.

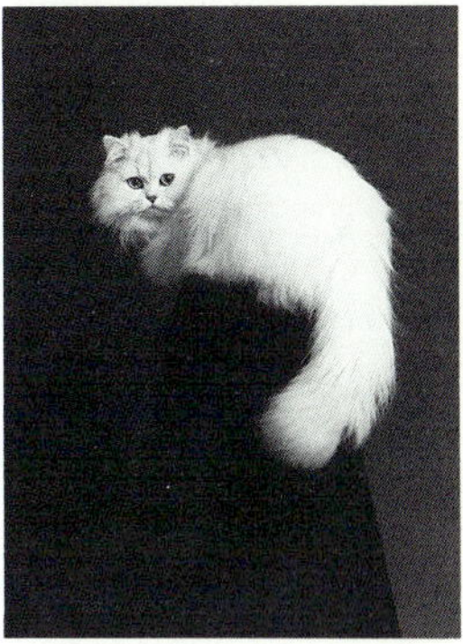

Black-And-White Film ▶
Monochrome gives your cat pictures a "traditional" look, and is specially easy to process and print in the home darkroom.

USING FLASH

With a flash unit on top of your camera, you can photograph a cat almost anywhere—even a black one in a coal cellar! Most flash units are small enough to fit into your pocket, yet they give out a remarkably powerful burst of light, and operate on two or three small batteries. Your camera may even have a flash unit built-in.

Compared to other sources of artificial light, a flash unit has a few other advantages which are less obvious than power and convenience. The flash is virtually instantaneous, illuminating your cat like a flash of lightning for only a 1/1000 of a second or so. Since even a leaping cat moves an insignificant distance in this time, photographs taken by flash show no trace of movement blur. Flash is cool light, too, so unlike a light bulb, it will not make your cat uncomfortably warm. Finally, the burst of light from a flash unit is daylight-colored, so pictures taken on regular film come out with natural hues.

Flash and Your Camera

Before using flash, always consult the manual supplied with the unit. If flash is built into your camera, you usually need only push a switch or button to start taking flash photographs. When camera and flash are separate, though, you'll need to do a little more. First, check that the flash unit is switched off, then slide its foot into the "hot-shoe" atop the camera.

Older cameras that lack a hot shoe must be connected to the flash using a cord. Plug this into the small round socket (usually marked 'x') on the camera body.

Unless you have a dedicated flash unit (see right) you will have to set the camera's shutter dial to a speed marked X, marked in red, or a lightning-bolt symbol. You can use this shutter speed, or any slower one. If you cannot find any special marking, set the dial to 1/60.

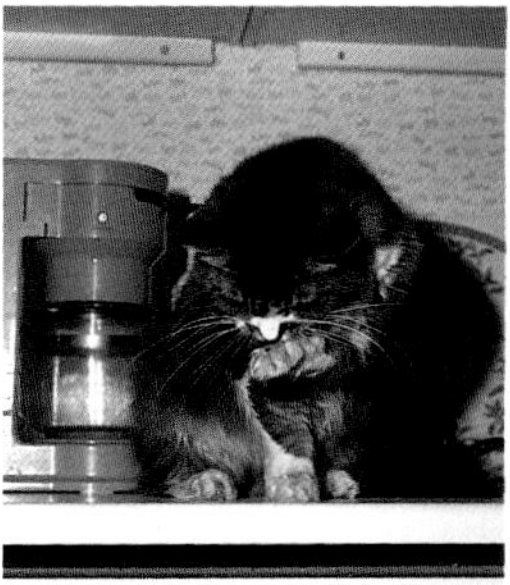

Dedicated Flash ▲

Some "intelligent" flash units exchange information with the camera. These dedicated flashguns make flash pictures like this one very simple—for example, most set the camera to the correct shutter speed for flash, but switch back to available light mode while the flash unit recycles. Details vary, so consult the instruction book for more information.

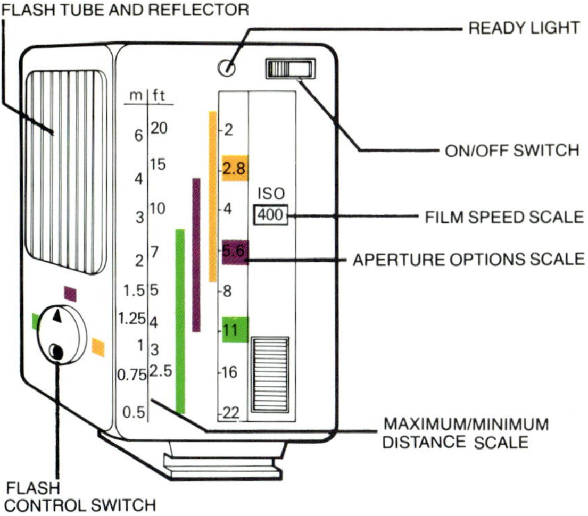

Exposure for Auto-Flash

You will find on the flash unit a calculator dial similar to the one shown here—locate on it the film speed index, and set this to the ISO value of the film in the camera. Now look for an aperture scale, to see which apertures you can use—they are usually marked with color.

For each choice of aperture, there is a range of possible subject distances (shown here by colored stripes). You must make sure that your cat is within the subject range allowed for the aperture you have chosen—otherwise exposure will be inaccurate.

Finally, set the aperture option you have chosen on the camera's lens, and on the flash control switch. This is often located at the front of the unit. After switching the flash on, you're ready to take pictures. After taking one, watch the "ready-light" on the unit. This goes out while the flash unit recycles, and when it relights you can take another photograph.

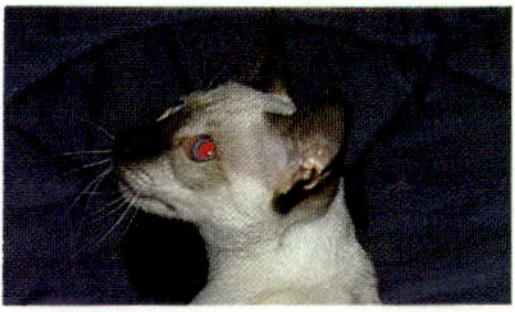

Avoiding Red-Eye ▲

The eyes of cats often glow red in flash photographs. You can avoid this in several ways: by shining a flashlight at the cat just before taking the picture; by moving the flash well away from the camera on an extension cable; or by bouncing the flash light off the ceiling, as explained on page 59.

WHAT ELSE DO YOU NEED?

Besides a camera and of course a cat, is there anything else that will help you to take good pictures? The most important things are those you cannot buy: a keen observant eye, time, and above all patience and understanding. There are, however, a few accessories that can be of some help. A flash unit is most useful, and comparatively cheap to buy.

If you own an SLR camera, you may want to buy different lenses for it as your skill and enthusiasm increase. Zoom lenses are particularly valuable, because they make it easier for you to keep the cat neatly framed as it moves around, and most also have a "macro" setting which enables you to move in close. On page 78 you'll find more about lenses and how they can enliven your cat pictures.

The most valuable accessory of all, though, is experience. Photography is a bit like learning to play the piano: buying the instrument is just the beginning. If you use your camera only rarely, you'll not only fumble with the controls, but you'll also find it hard to anticipate the cat's action and press the shutter release at just the right instant. But with more practice, you'll find that you get better and better pictures of your cat.

Filters

These are thin squares or circles of glass or plastic that fit in front of your camera's lens. The most useful is a skylight or UV filter, which protects your lens from dirt and scratches. If you use color negative film, you will rarely need to use any other filter, because the film is so tolerant of variations in the color of light. But with slide film, you will find a couple more filters quite useful. A straw-colored 81B filter removes the blueness that spoils pictures taken on a cloudy day; and a deep blue 80A filter takes much of the orange color out of pictures of your cat taken by the light of ordinary household lamps. This filter will also improve the colors of pictures taken on negative film in similar conditions.

A polarizing filter is useful, but again not essential, with either film type. Orientated correctly over the lens, it reduces glare and reflections, giving richer colors, and making skies look bluer.

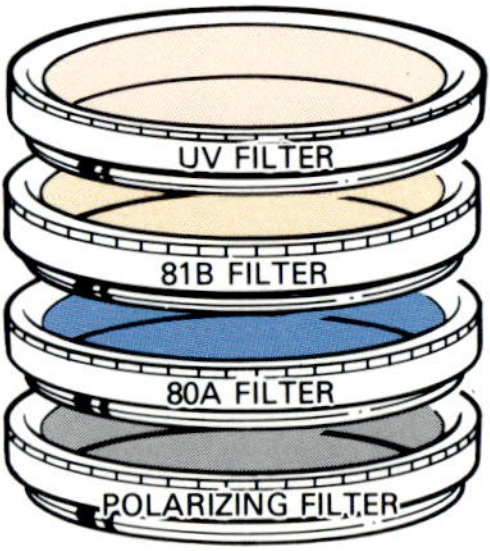

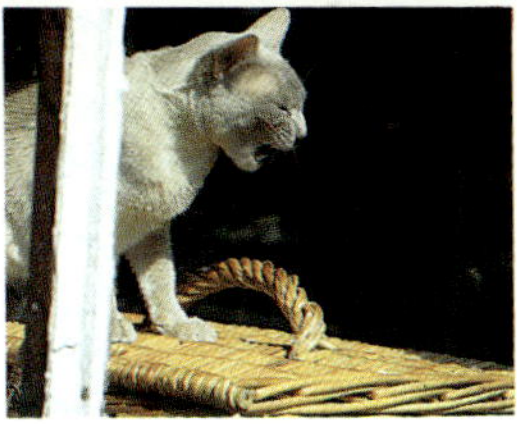

WITHOUT FILTER

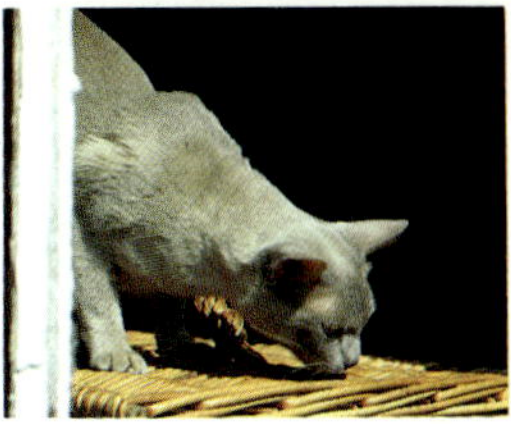

WITH POLARIZING FILTER

Removing Reflections

A polarizing filter removed the reflections on the glass in the picture above, making the cat more clearly visible.

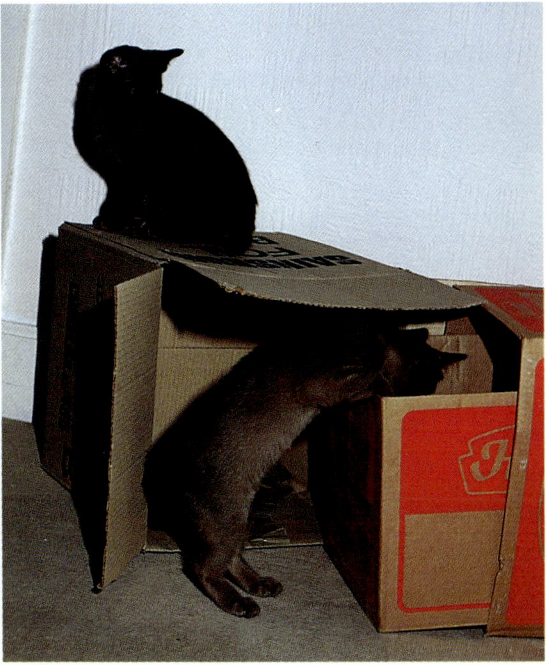

Feline Fun

Sometimes the most useful accessories are not photographic at all—a battered cardboard box occupied these cats for almost half an hour while the owner took pictures.

A FELINE PORTRAIT

If you've already tried making a portrait of your cat, you know that it doesn't seem easy at first attempt. Cats are totally individual, and from behind the camera, they often seem as fickle and hard to photograph as Hollywood stars. Some are the Marilyn Monroes of the cat world, preening and pouting for the photographer; others have more in common with Greta Garbo, and stalk off with a swish of the tail that surely says "I want to be alone."

The chapter that follows explains some of the ways that you can control these patterns of behavior, and even turn them to advantage. You'll also find here tips on purely photographic points, such as how to control daylight and artificial light to bring out your cat's markings and the shine in its coat.

Photo techniques and cat behavior aren't the only things to remember, though; your pictures will be better if you pay special attention to little details. A well-groomed cat always looks more attractive on film than one that has a dirty coat and grubby ears. You may need to take the time of year into consideration, too, as some cats look better in winter, and others in summer. All these points are covered in the next few pages.

However good you get at cat portraiture, you cannot expect every picture to be perfect, so think of the garbage bin as a helpful friend who accepts everything, and never criticizes. Carefully analyse why some pictures are better than others, and throw away your worst. One of the best ways of learning is through your own mistakes—but you don't have to keep the evidence.

In a Garden Studio

Perfect portraits needn't be ruthlessly formal: This elegant picture was taken while the cat took a break from rolling happily in the photographer's yard. She rustled a nearby plant with her foot to attract her pet's attention and provoke an alert expression.

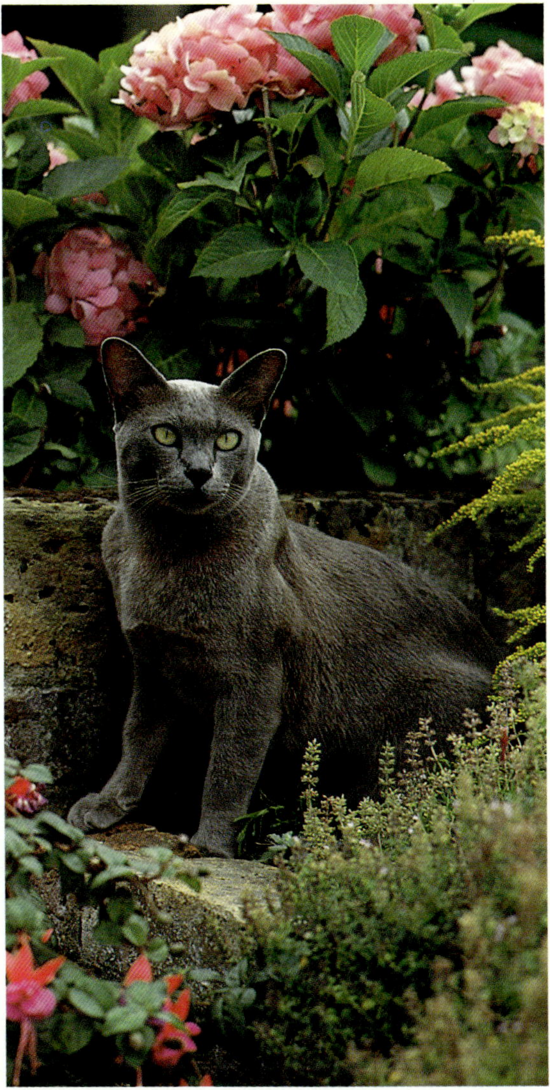

CAT CARE FOR THE CAMERA

Cats are fastidiously clean creatures, and spend a good part of their day washing themselves. A well-fed, healthy cat will have bright, clear eyes, and a gleaming coat, but some breeds, especially those with long coats, need a helping hand to look really sparkling.

If the coat is very dirty, or the fur matted, you may have to bathe the cat, as explained below. Usually, though, all that is needed is a little grooming. Long-haired breeds have very soft, fine coats which benefit from being dusted with talcum powder. This adds body to the fur, making it fluff out. Use ordinary baby powder, rubbing it in well, then brushing it out. Pay particular attention to the ruff around the neck, brushing forward towards the head to give the cat a full-cheeked expression. Groom the tail downwards from the tip to the base of the spine: this will make it look full and bushy.

Even short-haired cats look better on film if you groom them for their photo-session. Use a fine comb or rubber brush to remove dead hair, then bring out the sheen with a final polish using a piece of silk, velvet or chamois leather. Dark-coated cats can have a little Bay Rum massaged into their fur. This will make the coat positively gleam, and it smells nice, too.

Bathing Your Cat

Cats hate water, so use a bath only as an extreme measure. Use warm water, not hot, and choose a special pet shampoo, making sure that none of it gets in the cat's eyes. Long-haired breeds will also benefit from a little hair conditioner before the final rinse.

Some cats do not like the sound or feeling of a hair-dryer, but if your pet does not mind, you can use one to speed drying, provided you keep the nozzle at least 18 inches (0.5 m) from the cat. The alternative is to towel it dry in a warm spot. During drying tease out small

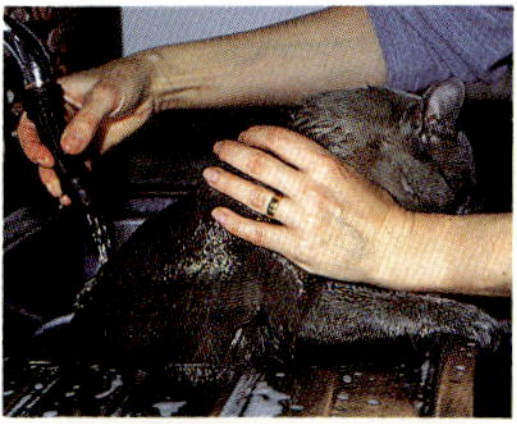

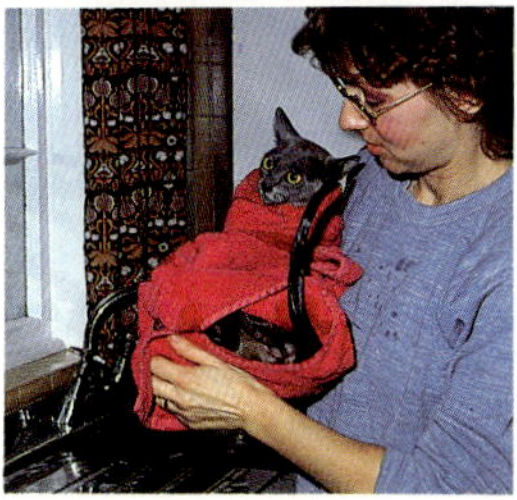

tangles, and comb or brush the cat periodically.

Stubborn matted fur is best untangled while the cat is still wet with conditioner. If there are any bits you cannot untangle, snip them away with blunt-tipped scissors—cut down through the knot, not across it.

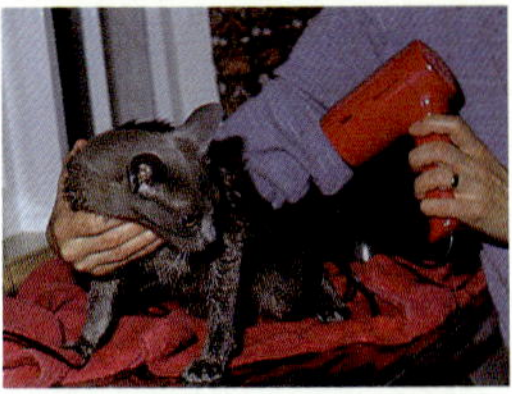

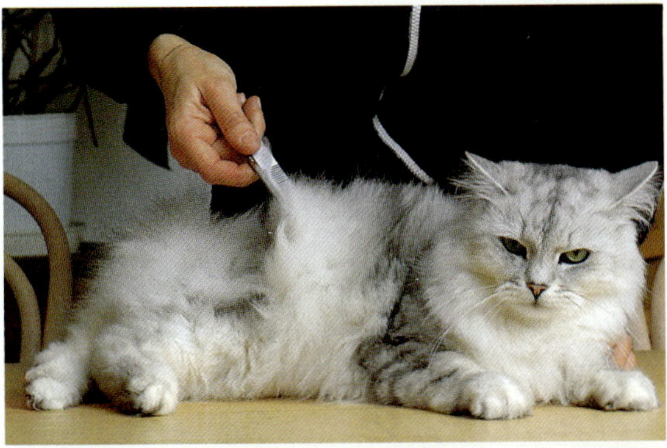

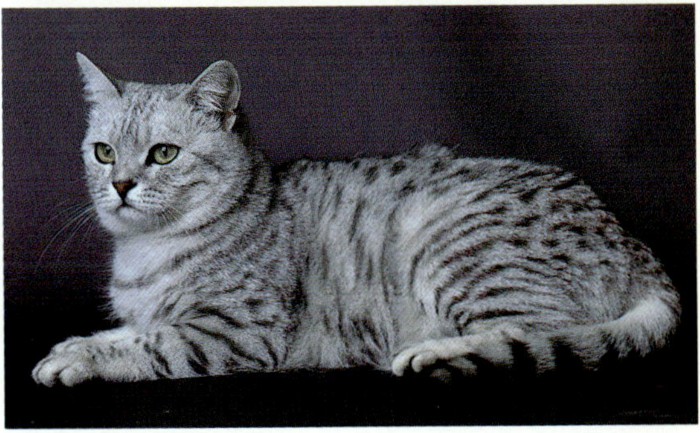

Details That Count

As a finishing touch, check your cat's eyes, ears and nose. These delicate areas should be cleaned with a cotton swab—though you may need a helper to hold the cat. The addition of a little drop of olive oil can help clean out the ears, but remember not to delve too far into the ear.

TIME OF YEAR

Like most other animals, cats show varying characteristics as the seasons change. The annual cycle is most pronounced in cats living out of doors; house cats that spend most or all of their time in a temperature-controlled environment may not display the changes of coat or behavior to nearly the same extent.

From a photographic point of view, the most important annual change is in the cat's coat—particularly with long-haired breeds. In the winter, these cats will have thick, luxuriant coats, and will look more photogenic as a result. As the weather gets warmer, the cat will start to molt, and by the summer months, the fur can be quite short, leaving the neck and tail as the only fluffy parts. The change in coat is less pronounced—though still noticeable—with shorter-haired breeds. Remember too that hairs that come off the cat don't just disappear—they stick to everything the cat touches. So when your cat is molting, groom it carefully, and avoid backgrounds that contrast strongly with its coat—or you will spend all your time picking fallen hairs off the background before taking the picture.

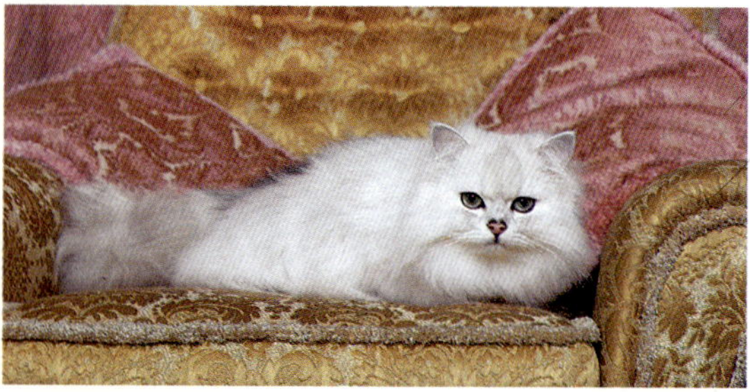

Seasonal Behavior ▲
Your cat's behavior changes at different times of year. This can sometimes make photography more difficult—but often easier, depending on the kind of photograph you want. In the spring, many breeds become frisky and playful, and it's pointless trying to get your cat to sit still for a formal portrait session when all it really wants to do is chase other cats around the garden! Equally, cold weather may make your cat sluggish and lethargic. This is the time to photograph her purring on the cushion in front of the fire as in this picture.

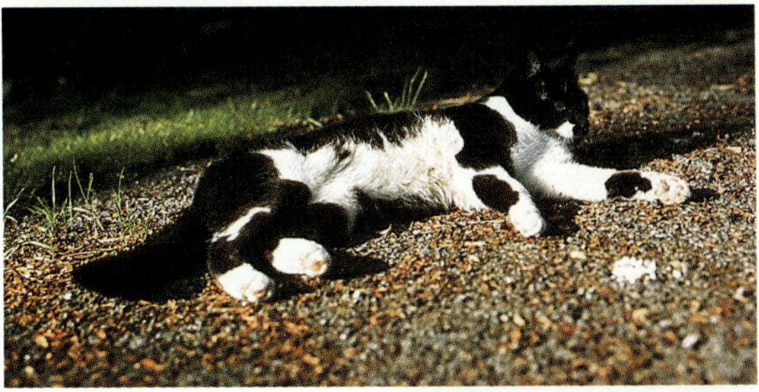

Pictures Outdoors
The spring and early summer months provide more outdoor photo opportunities. Most cats have a favorite basking place in the sun, as shown above and the cat's expression of contentment always makes a good picture. If you have a garden, it will be looking its best at these times—whereas in the heat of the summer, all but the most carefully-tended lawns form a parched brown background that does little to enhance your cat's appearance.

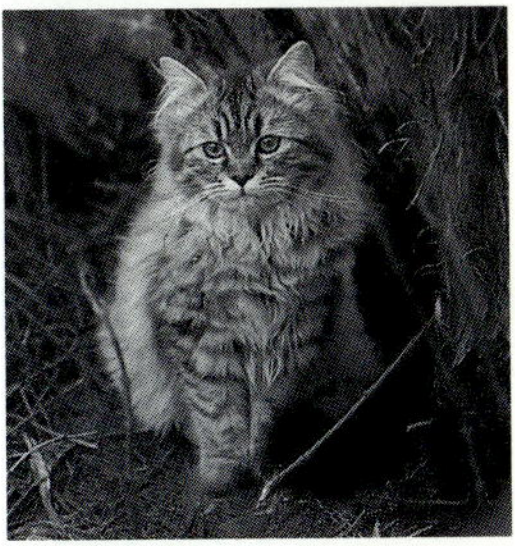

Closing In ▲
In arid conditions, close in to exclude parched foliage from the picture.

Seasonal Color ▼
Even when out of focus, spring foliage brightens up a picture.

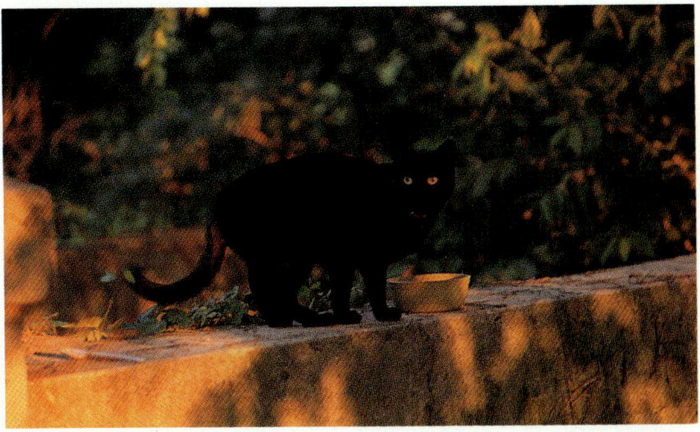

BREEDS AND PEDIGREES

There are well over eighty breeds of thoroughbred cats, including the associated color variations, but in terms of both character and appearance, this abundance of variety can be broadly arranged into five groups: Persians; American Shorthairs; Oriental Shorthairs; Burmese; and Siamese.

Some of these groups of cats present special photographic problems by virtue of their appearance, and cats within each group behave and react in a broadly similar way. If you plan to photograph any cat besides your own, or one that you know well, then it's worth learning a little about how these groups differ in shape and temperament. Forewarned is forearmed, and your chances of getting good pictures of a friend's cat are greatly increased if you know what to expect.

Burmese ▶

These cats have a similar temperament to Siamese—they are highly intelligent, and very active, and your biggest problem will be keeping them in one place—the hints on page 42 will help you do this. They love people, and will tend to run towards you, so use a telephoto lens, and keep your distance, or the cat will soon be at arm's length, peering into the lens.

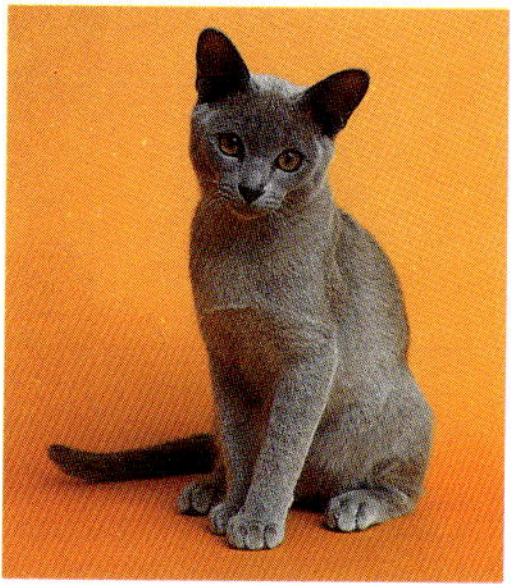

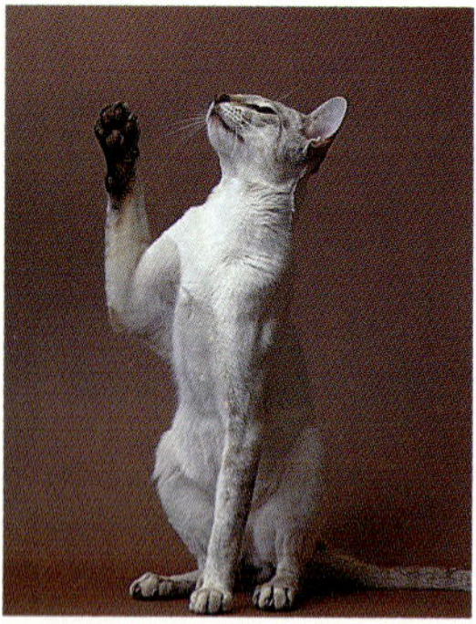

◀ Siamese

These are the original curious cats—they learn quickly, particularly where food is concerned, and will soon learn to open a cupboard door. They have long faces which often prove difficult to keep in focus from nose to ears—try increasing depth of field by using a small aperture, or, with non-adjustable cameras, take pictures in profile.

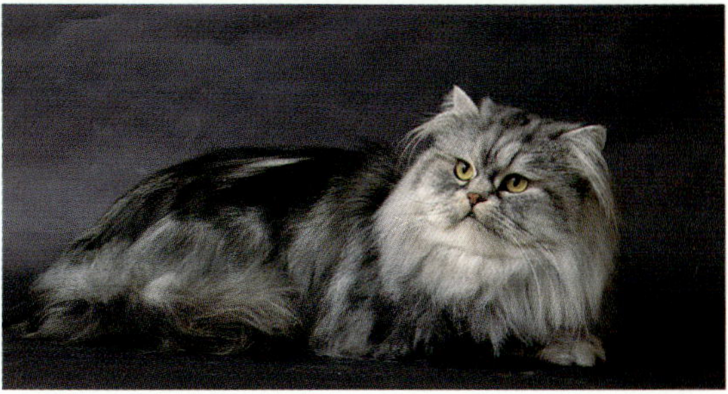

Persians

Some of the most beautiful cats fall into this category. Most are medium-sized, with a full coat, a short face, large round eyes and short ears. As adults, they are not terribly active, and you may have difficulty getting a Persian to look alert for the camera. Noise often animates them briefly—try a scratching sound, but be ready to take the picture while you have the cat's attention.

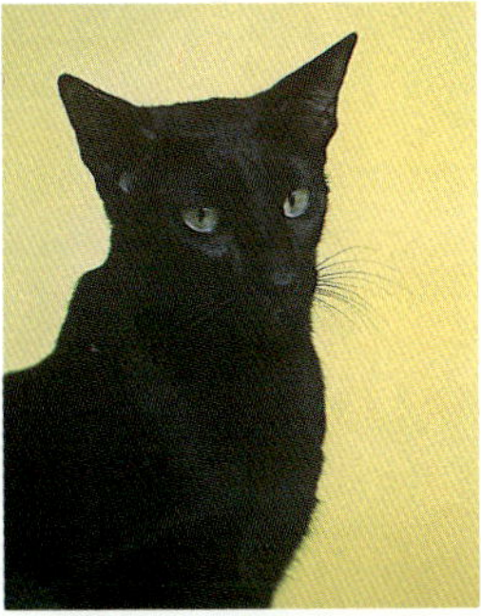

◀ Orientals

This group encompasses a tremendous variety of cats. Most have long slender bodies, large ears and sleek, close-lying fur. They are very playful cats, and you'll get your most characteristic photographs in bright light, where you can use a fast shutter speed to arrest their antics on film.

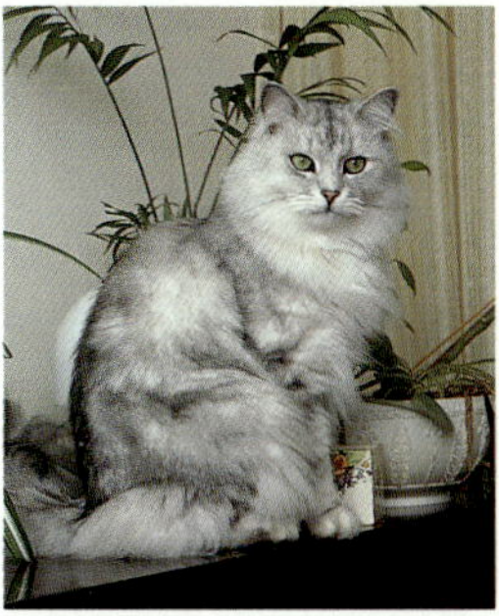

American Shorthair ▶

These are big strong cats, particularly if neutered, so you should have little difficulty making tightly-cropped portraits of them. They have quiet, gentle dispositions that make them ideal subjects for the novice photographer.

HABITS AND TRAINING

A cat's behavior may to the casual observer seem completely random and unpredictable, but cats, like people, are creatures of many fixed habits. If you take the time to watch your cat playing or going about its day-to-day business, you'll soon spot the same activity repeated time and time again.

As any aspiring cat photographer knows, though, seeing a cat perform a particularly attractive or humorous routine, and catching that same action on film are two quite different things. Most cats have a keen sense of irony, and it often seems as if they pride themselves on keeping you waiting, and never performing for the camera.

In reality, though, cats do have a schedule that is as fixed as the diary of any business executive. If you want to photograph your cat yawning, or perhaps washing, observe its timetable. A cat will usually follow a sequence of activity that runs . . . eat, wash, sleep, wake, stretch, yawn, play, eat, and so on. With this knowledge, all you need do is watch and wait with your camera ready, and the controls preset. Other types of feline behavior follow a similar pattern—though perhaps not such a predictable one.

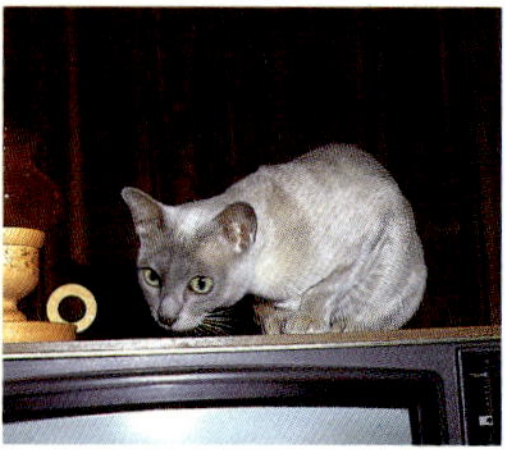

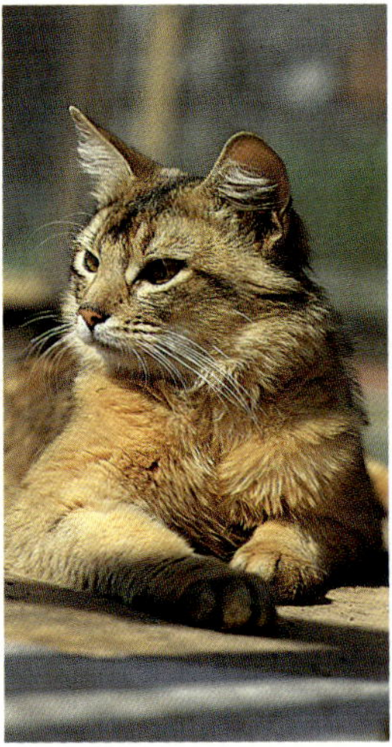

Attentive Cats

Cats love watching activity, and if you want pictures of your pet concentrating intently on something other than the camera, then one useful trick is to put the cat in a viewpoint that overlooks a busy spot. An obvious example is by a window—particularly if this overlooks a garden with birds in it.

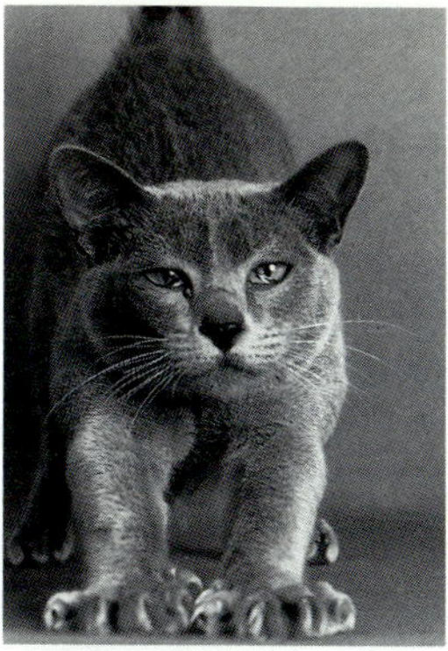

Waking Up
Nudge your sleeping cat for character-filled pictures of stretches and yawns.

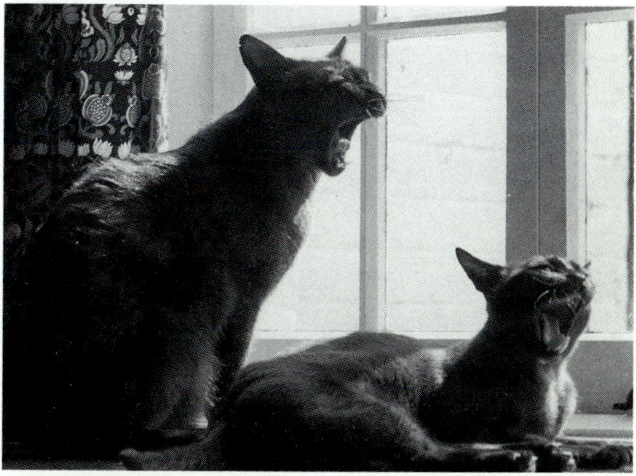

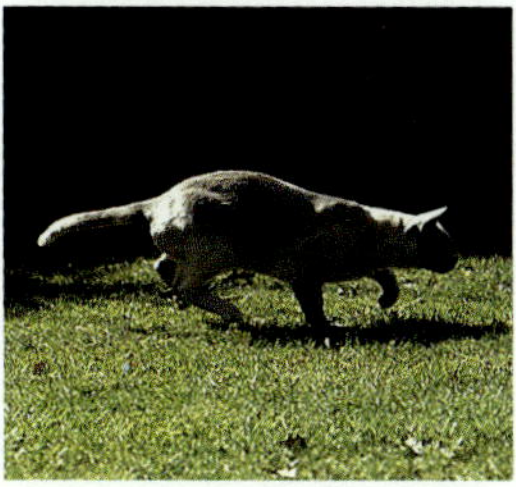

Get Your Cat Moving
Generally, a cat will run towards its owner when called, so many of your pictures probably show the cat from the front. To take side views, enlist some help from a friend—preferably someone the cat knows and likes. They can then call the cat, while you stand aside and take pictures.

Cats as Mimics

A few cats watch and copy their owners' actions. This cat had seen its owner picking up the receiver of the ringing telephone, and soon learned to do the same. To take this picture, the photographer arranged for a neighbor to call her, and stood by with the camera.

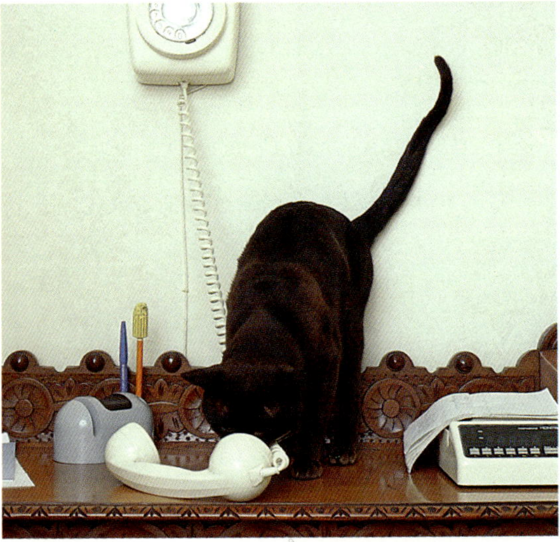

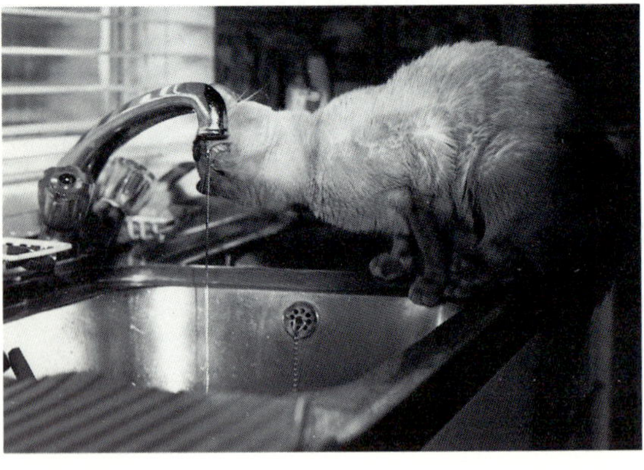

Conditioning Your Cat

Unlike dogs, cats cannot really be trained to do tricks for the camera such as rolling over, begging, or playing dead. The result will be frayed tempers and frustration, both for you and the cat, as you try to attain the impossible. However, if you have enough time and patience, you may be able to condition your cat to behave the way you want it to. For example, any cat-owner knows that a saucer rattled at feeding time soon brings a cat running, and a similar principle can be used to provoke more complex rituals, too.

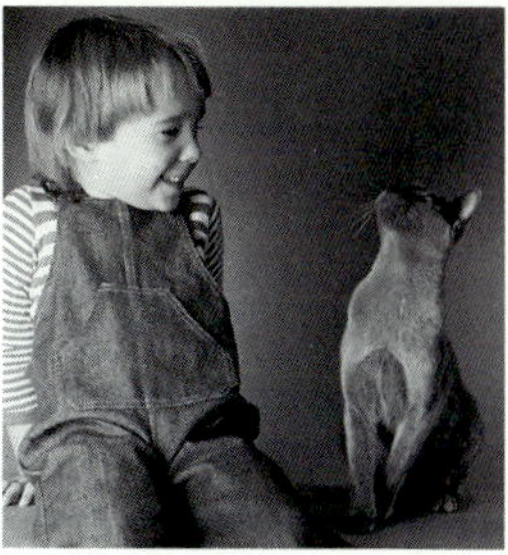

Making Friends ▲

Cats reserve a special welcome for their best friends: be ready with a camera to catch these magic moments.

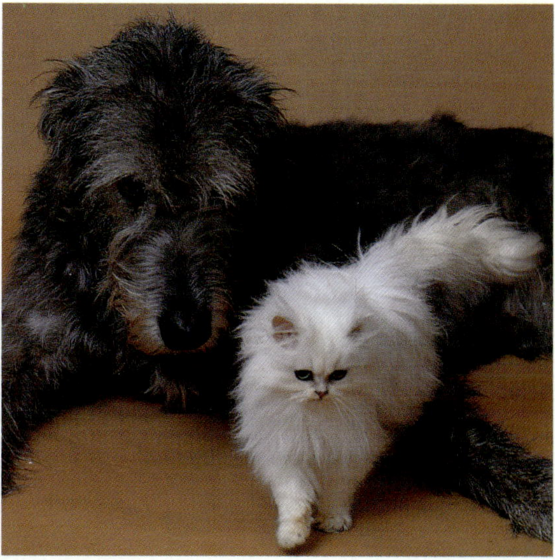

◀ Secret Drinker

Careful observation of your cat's habits will soon give you lots of ideas for pictures.

Fighting Like Cat and Dog ▲

With training and patience, traditional enemies will settle down together for a picture.

RESTRICTING MOVEMENT

Cats are such active, inquisitive creatures that you may have difficulty keeping yours in one place for long enough to make a good portrait. There are a few obvious steps you can take to stop your subject wandering off, such as shutting all doors and windows, but you might also try the techniques described below.

If none of these works, and your cat refuses to keep still, try using food as a bribe or as a calming influence, or else consider postponing your picture session until your model is in a less highly-strung mood.

Using Heat

Cats love heat, and will curl up comfortably in a warm place. Usually, though, they choose a spot such as an old heating radiator, which is not particularly photogenic. To get them where you want them, use a water bottle, a pet heater or an electric blanket. Cover the heated area with a piece of fabric or a blanket so that it is not visible. If you are using a hot-water bottle, make sure that it is only half full, or it will appear lumpy in your photos.

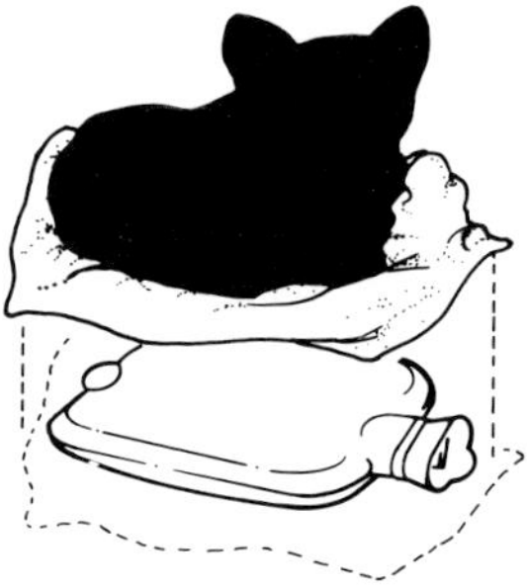

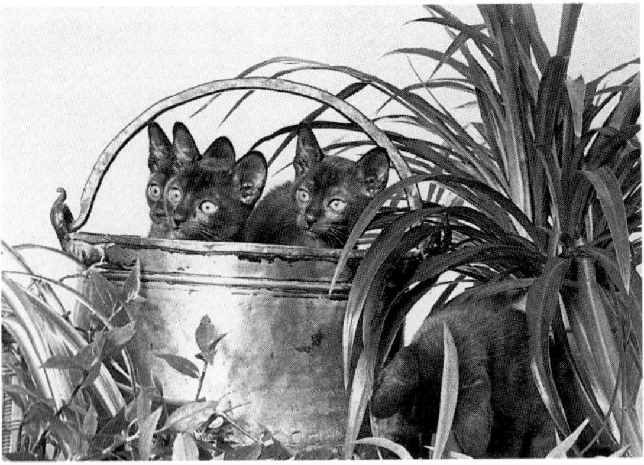

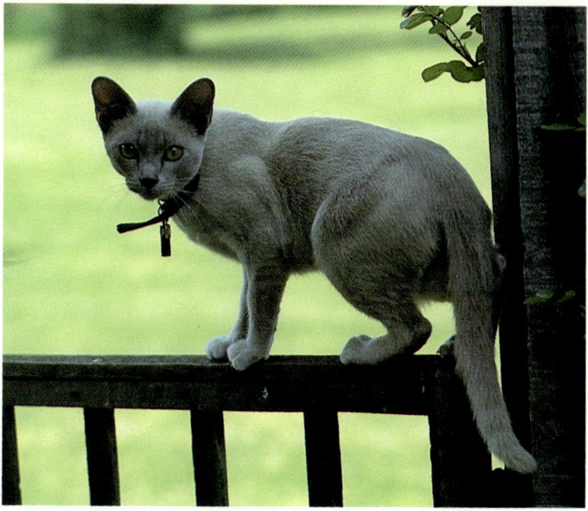

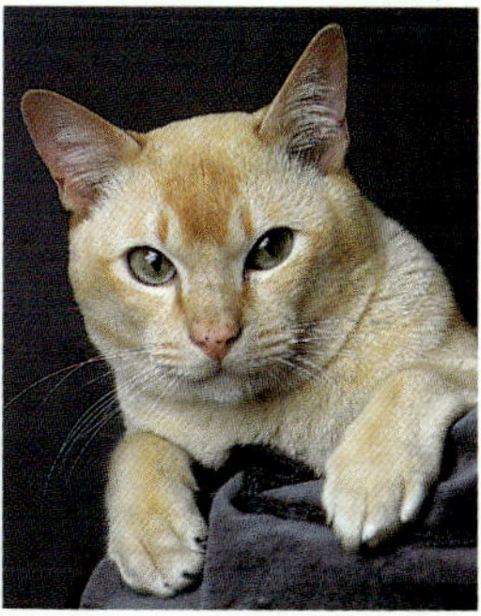

On a Shoulder ▲

Nervous cats may relax only when close to their owners. Photograph them in crossed arms, or over shoulders.

A Bucket of Cats

Try using containers to physically restrain your subjects.

Using Height ▲

Cats are good leapers, but will hesitate and assess the distance before launching off a perch—and you can take your picture during this moment's delay. A small table about 3 feet (1 m) high, or a wooden platform screwed onto a regular camera tripod will help to keep the cat in one spot. Cover this "cat stand" with a piece of fabric before taking pictures. Out of doors, you can use branches of trees for the same purpose.

Herbal Remedies

If you have a garden, plant catnip (Nepeta cataria). Cats will roll in it, chew it, and thoroughly enjoy it. You can even make use of sprigs indoors—placed under a piece of fabric, the herb will keep your cat interested and sniffing while you take pictures.

USING FOOD

Food motivates cats more strongly than almost anything else, and you can use food to keep your cat in front of the lens, or to persuade it to behave. This doesn't mean starving your pet for two days before taking pictures—it's more a matter of scheduling the picture-taking just before regular feeding time. Remember also that you should never tease a cat by offering a bribe and then not delivering the goods; this is cruel, and most unfair to a trusting pet. Equally, do not overdo the food bribes, or you could end up with a fat cat!

Cats' Reaction to Food ▼

You can use food in various ways. Anticipation of a snack will make the cat's eyes large and bright; the whiskers will point forward and the nose will twitch, producing a very alert expression. Food is therefore a particularly useful way to get an attractive response from the less demonstrative breeds, such as Persians. Many cats will jump up, trying to get the food from your hand. This will give you the chance to photograph them on their hind legs.

An unattractive effect of food is that it may make your cat drool. This often goes unnoticed at the time of taking the picture, and after the film is processed, it is too late to do anything. Keep some tissues handy to wipe the cat's mouth.

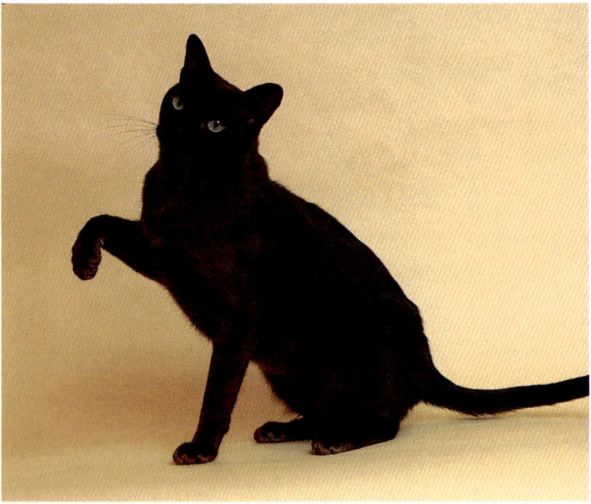

Buttering Up Your Cat

You can use small bits of butter as a versatile photo-aid. Smear it on, and your cat will almost immediately lick it off, so not only can you get pictures of your cat apparently washing itself, but you can also control where it licks. Try buttering one paw, for an attractive picture like the one at right or butter its lips to get it licking.

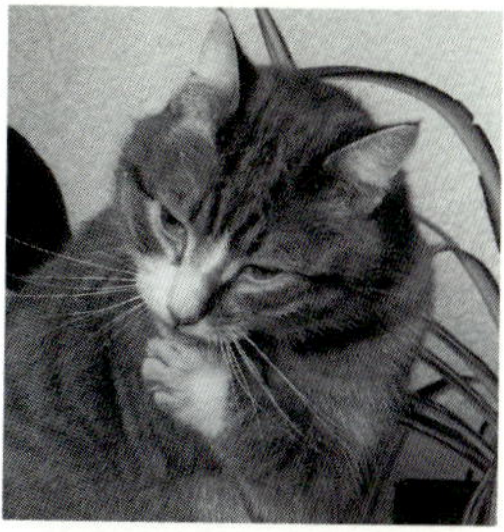

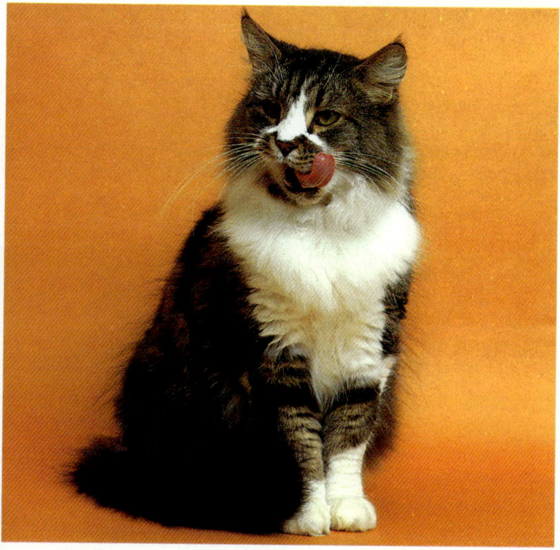

Which Food?

No two cats are the same in their tastes, and it is a matter of trial and error to discover which food generates the most photogenic response. Some types of food, though, are unsightly, and most are unidentifiable on film, provoking comments like "What's the cat got in its mouth?" You should therefore particularly avoid using messy, wet, oily or greasy foods that will stain either the background or the cat's coat.

Dried foods such as cat biscuits are probably best of all; very often the appearance or sound of the box will be enough to excite the cat, and get it looking in the right direction.

SETTINGS AND BACKGROUNDS

One of the factors that makes the difference between a snapshot of kitty and a real cat portrait is the background. All too often there is unwanted detail that makes the image confusing. And unless you picture your cat in its own habitat—whether this is the backyard or the house—there is a danger that the photos will look contrived and unnatural.

The general rule for backgrounds and settings is therefore "keep it simple". When preparing for a portrait session with your cat, it's best to clear away all moveable clutter, and pick an area where only plain surfaces are visible. Patterned carpets and wallpaper that appear tasteful and pleasing to the eye often seem ponderous and loud in photographs, and draw attention away from the cat. Patterned furnishing fabrics often have a similar effect.

Outdoor Settings

On a warm, dry day, most cats like to be out of the house to romp around the garden or balcony. Out of doors, you will have little trouble with lighting, too.

It is tempting to put the cat in front of a multi-colored flower bed, but as the picture at right shows, this often leads to garish pictures. Try to frame the cat against a single color of bloom, or against foliage or grass.

A garden may look its best in spring, but it can look good at other times of year, if you plant carefully. Pick late-flowering varieties, bulbs for early spring, and colorful shrubs for autumn and winter.

If your cat always lives indoors, don't try taking pictures on its first day in the "great outdoors." It is quite likely that strays and feral cats will have fought for territorial rights over your property and left their scent on it. Initially your own cat will feel like an intruder, and will relax only after it has had time to explore and stake its claim to the area.

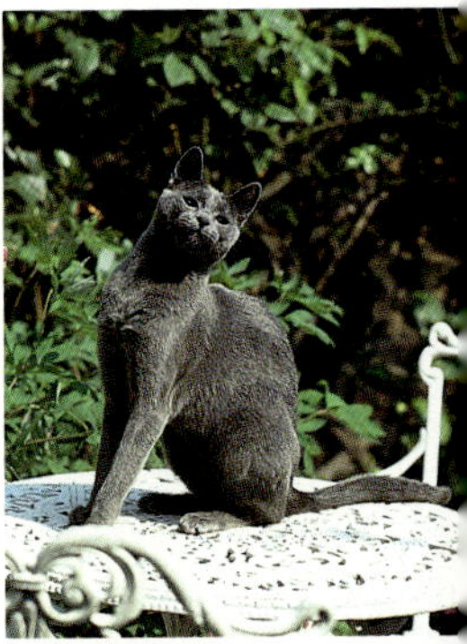

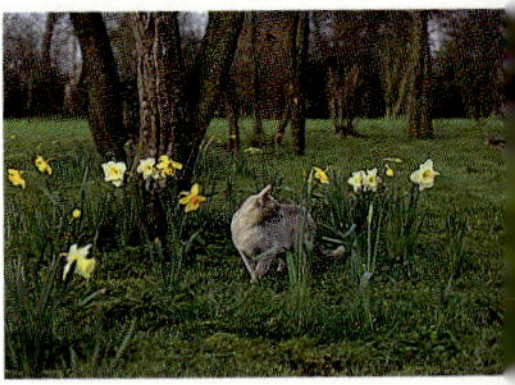

An Eye For Details

It's easy to be so absorbed in your primary subject—the cat—that you don't notice details in other parts of the frame. Many an otherwise lovely composition has been spoiled because the photographer failed to notice a tree in the background, and in the print this appears to grow out of the cat's head. There are many superfluous details indoors, too; electrical cables, telephones, TV antennae are all so much part of the domestic scene that they become almost transparent to the eye—but not to the camera. The observant photographer will watch out for and remove such distractions, or will move the camera to a different angle to avoid including them in the picture.

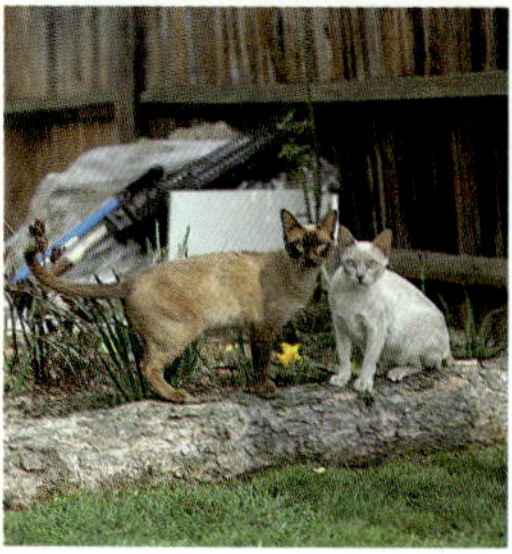

Appropriate Settings

If you find plain backgrounds too austere, then introduce one or two ornaments—but make sure they complement the cat.

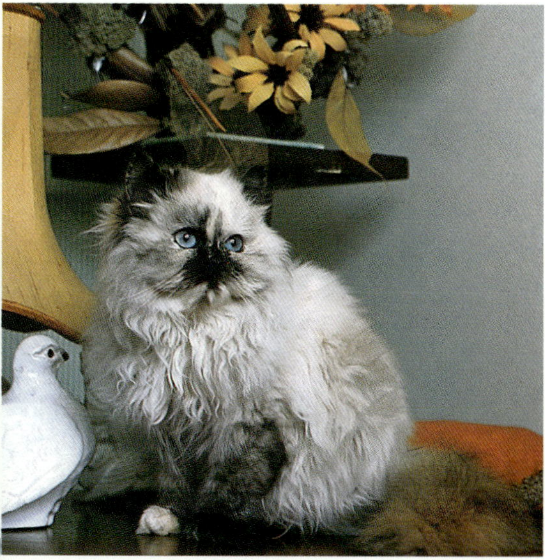

Previewing Depth of Field

Although the viewfinder of an SLR generally shows the scene exactly as it appears on film, these cameras have a major failing as far as backgrounds are concerned. Viewing is normally at full aperture, so the focusing screen is at its brightest. However, when the lens closes down to the working aperture preset by the photographer, more of the scene becomes sharp, and background details that were previously invisible suddenly appear clear and well-defined.

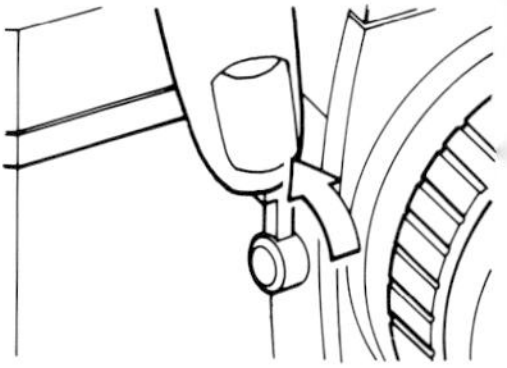

Most cameras have a depth-of-field preview control that closes the lens down to the working aperture, showing depth of field as it will appear on film. Use this to gauge how sharp the background will be in the photograph.

Special Backgrounds

For the perfect portrait, you may want to buy either fabric or paper as a background for your cat. Bolts of fabric are available in a tremendous variety of colors, patterns and textures from any department store, but you may not know about seamless paper. This is sold by photographic goods suppliers, and has a non-reflective surface. It generally comes wound on a cardboard tube nine feet long. The paper wound on the roll is therefore too wide for a single cat, and for economy it is probably best to saw the roll into halves. This also reduces the likelihood of creasing and solves storage problems.

The advantage of seamless paper is that you can drape it from a fixing point high on a wall above the cat, and down onto a flat horizontal surface such as a table-top. As the name suggests, the paper then forms a continuous sweep of unbroken background.

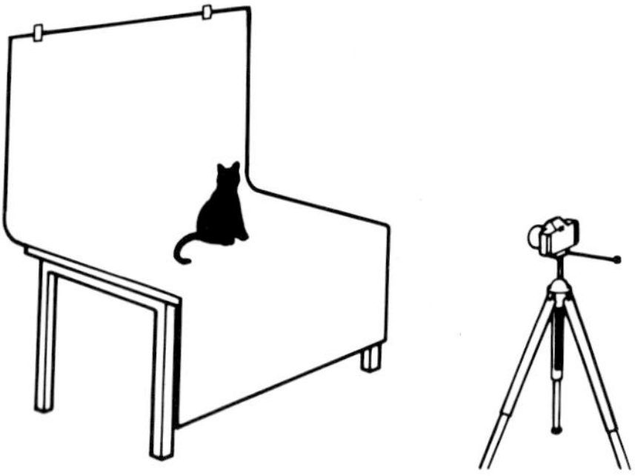

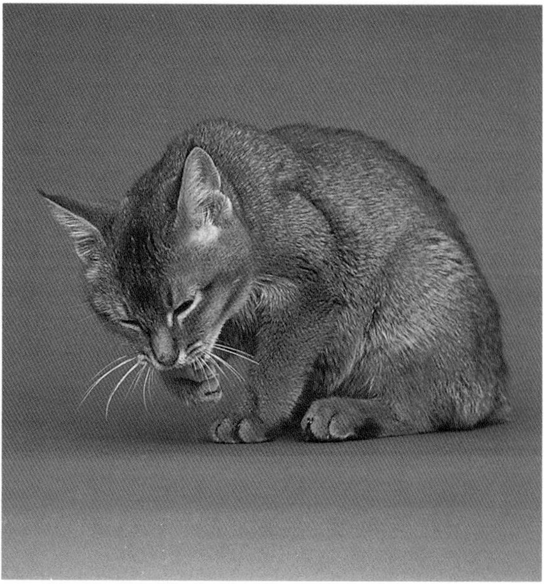

Background Color

Unless you're using black-and-white film, you should think carefully about the background hue. Choose one that complements the cat's coat and eye color, and try to avoid very bright backgrounds which draw attention away from the cat itself.

If you use color print film, you will find that bright backgrounds have another unwanted effect. They can mislead the machine that prints your photographs, so that the cat takes on a tinge opposite to the color of the background. A brilliant red backdrop, for example, might make your cat turn slightly cyan (greeny-blue). If this color shift is severe, ask for your pictures to be reprinted.

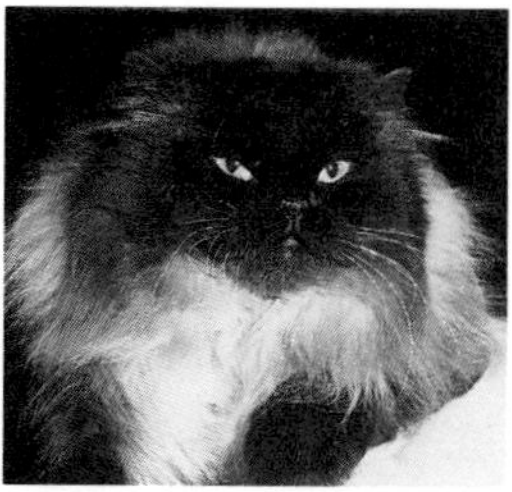

Plain Black Backgrounds

To produce a featureless black surround for your cat, use direct flash, and move the cat well clear of the background.

PROPS AND TOYS

Encouraging a cat to play isn't usually difficult: in the absence of anything real to toy with, many will amuse themselves with an imaginary companion, or simply chase their own tails. Small props, though, make useful aids in provoking play, and for getting the cat to pose attractively in front of the camera.

Pet stores sell many ready-made toys such as furry mice, and balls containing rice or bells. Some of the most effective toys, though, cost nothing. The best ones are those that make noises to attract your cat's attention, and those that remind it of birds or small animals that it would hunt in the wild. You needn't aim for a completely lifelike resemblance—this would, after all, look a little macabre on film! Cats have vivid imaginations, and will chase anything furry or fluffy, or that passes them with a jerking, unpredictable motion.

Whether you make a toy yourself, or simply choose a ready-made one, decide beforehand whether or not it will appear in the photograph. Appearance does not matter if the toy is to be held just off-frame, but if you are going to include it in the picture, the toy should look appropriate both to the setting and to the cat.

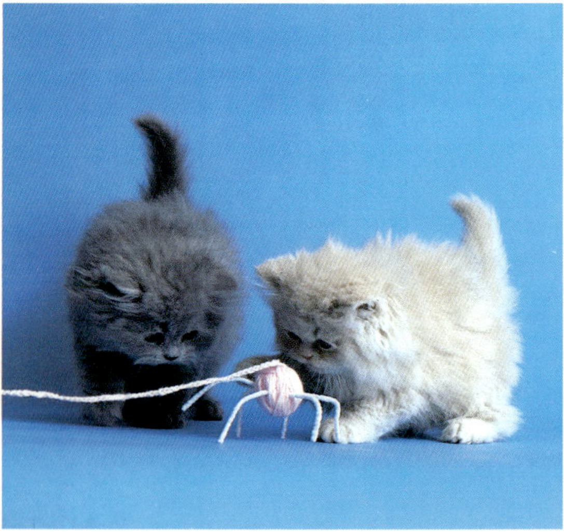

Using Toys

Toys that won't appear in the photo can be improvised from anything—even a 35 mm film canister or a crumpled piece of paper. Tie some twine on the toy—the cat's attention will be caught by the swinging object, and it will overlook the support. The cat will soon start to play, swatting the toy with its paw, or jumping up when you hold the toy out of reach.

If you have a helper, you can look through the camera's viewfinder while the other person plays with the cat. However, an equally satisfactory technique is to fix the camera onto a tripod, and look through the viewfinder at the start of the picture session to check what area of the background is within the frame. You may want to use adhesive tape to mark on the background the position of the frame corners. You can then take your eye away from the camera and play with the cat yourself, operating the shutter using a cable-release.

If you do this, be sure to compose the picture with plenty of space around the cat, otherwise its vigorous movements may take a paw or tail-tip out of the frame.

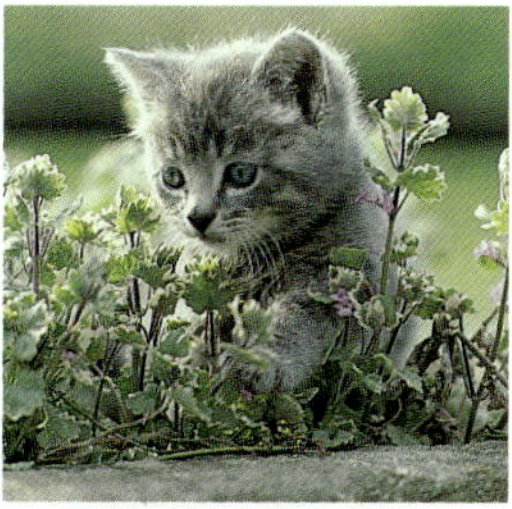

Eyes Left! ▲

Off-frame toys take a kitten's eyes off the camera.

◀ Interesting Props

If you think that the set you are using is too simple and austere, you may decide to add interest with a prop or accessory. Avoid the temptation to put too much in the picture, though, or you will draw attention away from the cat. Aim for appropriateness above all. Kittens, for example, look cute tangled in colorful balls of wool, but a fully-grown tomcat would just look stupid.

Catching Action ▼

Cats move very quickly when they jump to reach toys. Set a fast shutter speed, or use a flash unit as explainea on page 90.

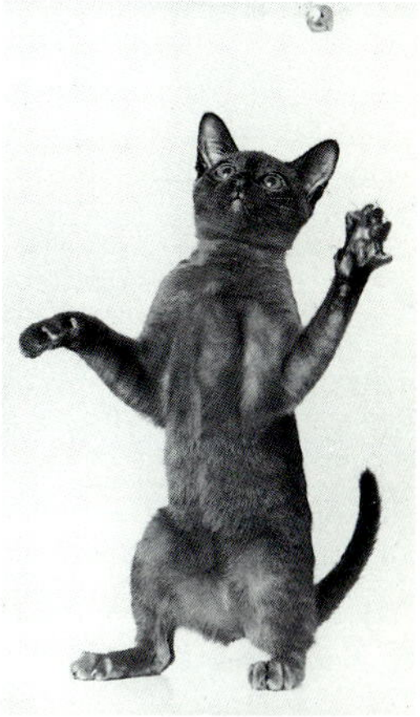

LIGHTING OUTDOORS

Out of doors, there's light in abundance—even on a cloudy day the light is much brighter outdoors than inside. So in the yard or on the porch it's easy to take natural-looking pictures of your cat, regardless of your level of expertise, or the complexity of your camera.

However, the sun's direct rays can sometimes be harsh and unflattering, and to make the most of sunlight you may need to use simple reflectors, such as sheets of newspaper, to throw light into the shadows hiding detail on your cat. There are other techniques, too, that you will find useful when taking outdoor pictures of your cat. Perhaps the most surprising is the use of flash. In brilliant sunshine, your camera's built-in or accessory flash unit can put sparkle into your cat's coat, and "catch-lights" into its eyes, as explained on page 55.

Lighting Direction

The quality of daylight varies from season to season, and even from hour to hour. During spring and fall the sun is low in the sky, whereas in midsummer it is overhead for much of the day, creating unflattering shadows. During the summer, therefore, it is better to take pictures only in the early morning and late afternoon, when the sun is closer to the horizon as shown at right.

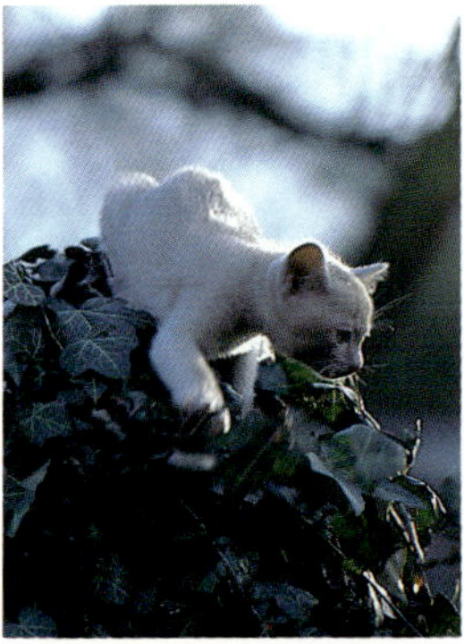

The conventional wisdom for taking snapshot pictures is "make sure the sun is behind your left shoulder." This advice produces front lighting that displays your cat's markings to best advantage, but also makes the cat squint. A better approach is to stand with the sun at your side, so that the cat is sidelit, as in the picture at right.

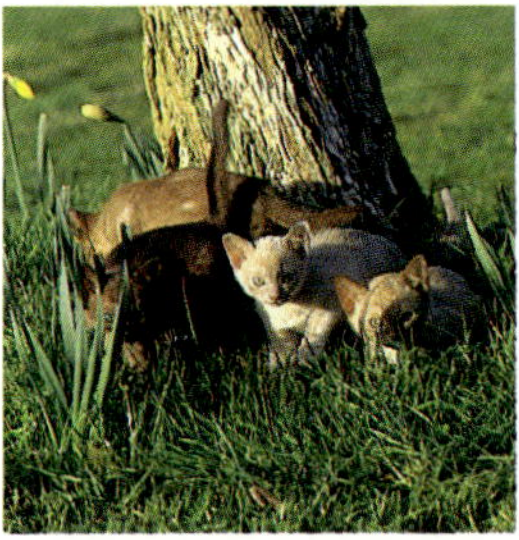

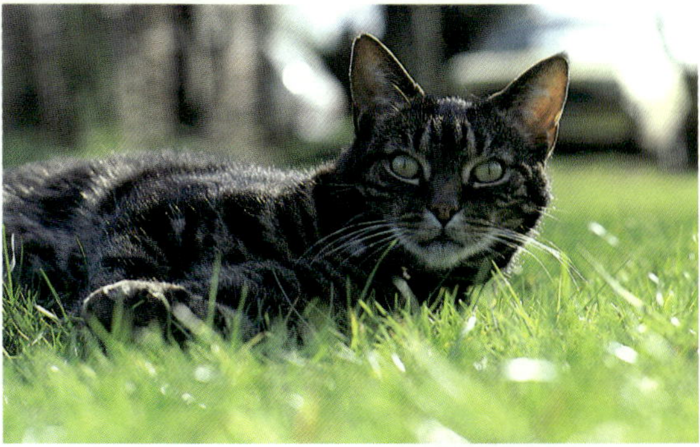

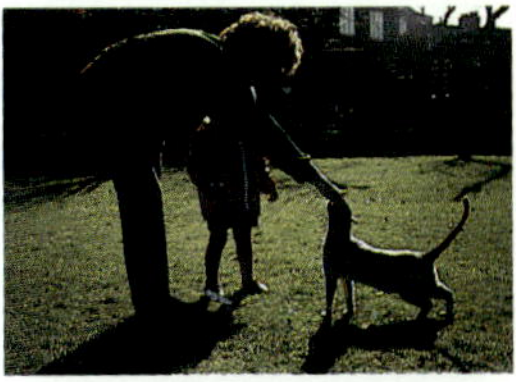

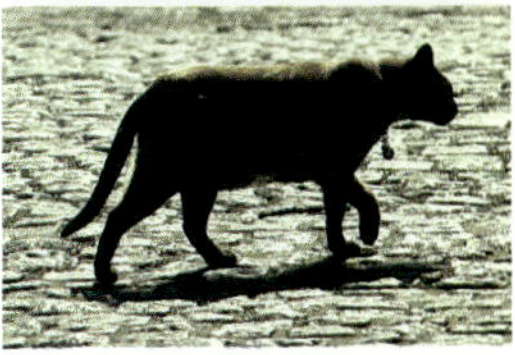

Backlighting

Backlighting surrounds your cat with a ring of light. Create it by putting the cat on a fence or tree-branch, so that it's shadow falls towards the camera. Take special care with exposure, or your camera may be misled by the bright background. If your camera has a backlight control, operate this to give extra exposure, or alternatively, use fill-in flash as explained overleaf. If you have the option of manual control, move near enough to the cat so that its shaded side fills the frame, note the settings that the meter indicates, and set these on the camera's controls before moving back to recompose the picture. If your camera has a "memory hold" button, use this to make the procedure easier. Backlit and sidelit pictures can be greatly improved if you use a reflector, as described on the next page.

Making Silhouettes

Prowling cats make graphic shapes, and if you have an adjustable camera you can deliberately record the cat's shape as a silhouette. The technique works best with dark-furred cats. Put them on a tree branch or fence, so that they appear backlit against a bright sky. Alternatively, frame the cat against the light reflected from water or wet paving, as in this picture. Take a meter reading from the bright background to set exposure.

Controlling Sunlight

Photographic film is capable of recording only a limited range of brightness. Those that fall outside the range will appear burned-out to white, or inky black. If you use a reflector to bounce light into the shadows, you will reduce the range of brightness and your pictures will look more colorful, and less harsh.

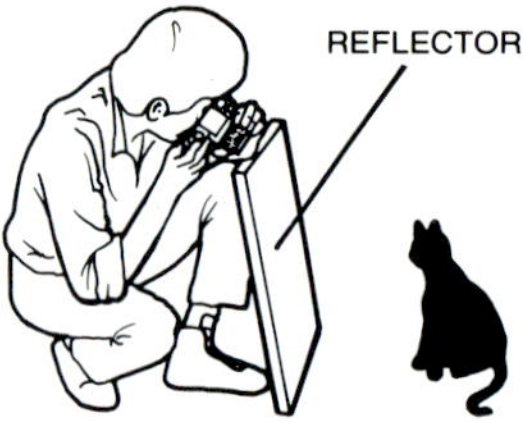

Anything white makes a good reflector—you can even improve sunlit close-ups by wearing white clothing. The most convenient reflector, though, is a piece of stiff white cardboard. Shift its angle while looking through the camera's viewfinder, to see how the light it reflects improves the appearance of your cat.

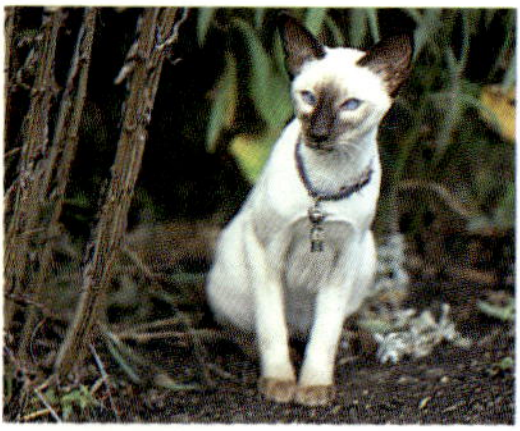

In the Shade

There is one other way to soften the harsh shadows cast by bright sun—simply move the cat into the shade, and take pictures there.

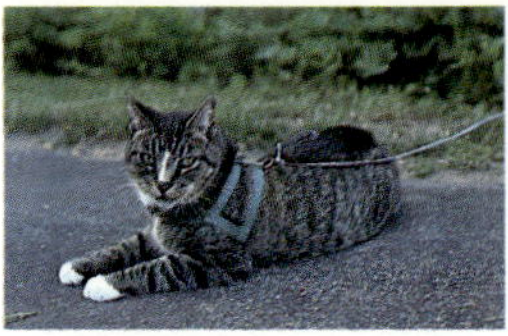

NO FILTER

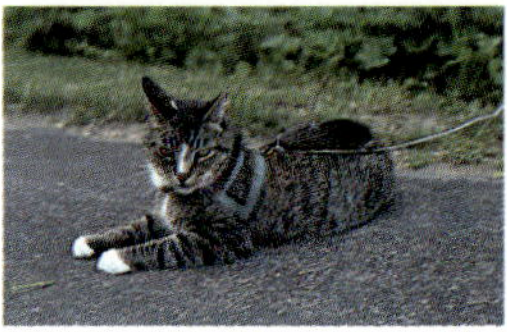

WITH 81B FILTER

Using Filters

If your camera has a threaded ring around its lens, you'll find that you can get more colorful pictures in sunshine by using a polarizing filter. The filter's effect depends on its position: with SLRs, simply fit the filter and rotate it; you'll see in the viewfinder which orientation brings about the most improvement. With other cameras, turn the filter in front of your eye, and note when the scene looks best. Maintain the same angle in fitting the filter to the camera.

If you use slide film, there is another filter that can improve your pictures: in dull weather, or if the cat is in the shade when the sky is blue, use a straw-colored 81B filter for truer hues.

WITHOUT FILTER

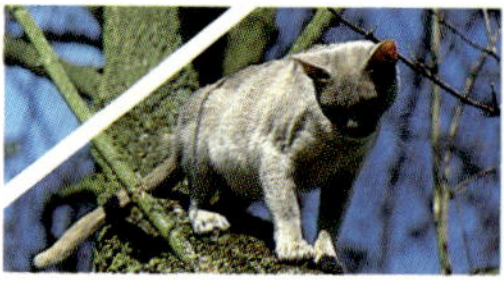

WITH POLARIZING FILTER

FILL-IN FLASH

If you have a flash unit, you'll find it as useful outdoors by day as it is inside. In sunny weather, you can use the flash to put extra light into the shadows of the picture, so that contrast is reduced. This will lead to clearer more colorful highlights in the print, and brighter, more detailed shadow areas. On a dull day, flash adds a sparkle to your cat's coat, and puts a twinkle in its eye.

With a simple camera that has a built-in flash, just switch it on, and use the camera as normal. If in the resulting pictures the background looks too dark, as if the picture was taken at night, tape a double layer of tissue over the flash reflector and try again.

With flash units for SLR cameras you need to follow a special procedure. For best results in sunlight, use a film with a speed of ISO 100 or lower. If you have a dedicated flash unit, refer to your flash manual for the correct procedure.

1 Mount the flash on the camera; set the flash-shutter speed on the camera—usually 1/60 second.

2 Set an automatic flash to manual (or make it act like a manual unit by covering its light sensor with your finger when you release the shutter).

3 On the flash, set the ISO setting to double that of the film you are using. Keep the camera set at the film's actual ISO rating.

4 As usual, set the lens aperture according to the meter reading.

5 On the flash calculator dial, find the distance that corresponds to the lens aperture you just set.

6 Stand this distance from your pet and take the picture.

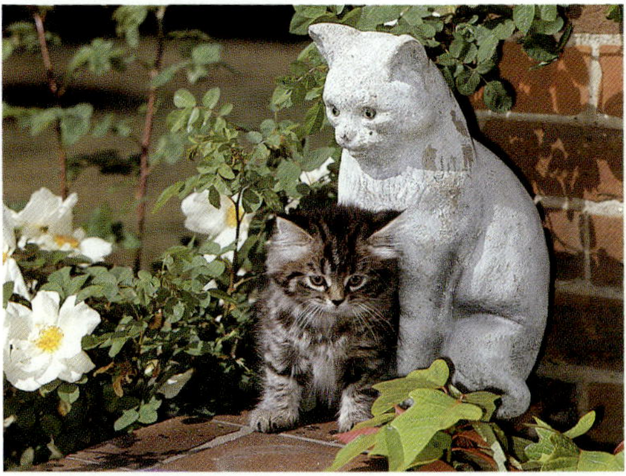

LIGHTING INDOORS

In the home, you have a choice of three different light sources when photographing your cat: daylight; electronic flash and bulb flash (flash cubes or flip-flash); and regular household lights such as table lamps or fluorescent tubes. Each light source has its own characteristic qualities, as explained below, and you'll have to adapt your technique as you switch from one to the other.

Commonly used films are known as daylight films because they are designed to give truest colors when used with daylight or its equivalent, electronic flash. Household (tungsten) and fluorescent bulbs yield light of a different color than daylight, a fact not readily perceived by the eye, but inescapable to film. Thus, pictures taken under tungsten lighting appear orangish, and those taken under fluorescent lighting may show a tinge of green. As we shall shortly see, these tinges can be minimized if you find them unacceptable.

Using Window Light

Move your cat close to the window, and you can take pictures more or less as you would out of doors. Most times of the day, and with all but the slowest of films, window light is bright enough to enable you to use quite a fast shutter speed, so there is no risk of camera-shake spoiling the pictures.

Window light is strongly directional, and this can be both an advantage and a drawback. Soft directional lighting is very flattering to a cat, provided the shadows it creates are not too dark. On the other hand, in a large room, or one decorated in dark tones, your cat will appear very brightly lit on one side, and in deep shadow on the other—particularly if sunlight is streaming in from outside.

To get the best out of a window, then, use reflectors to fill in the shadows. If you position the camera between the cat and the window, you'll have the ideal light for close-up pictures; the cat's eyes reflect the rectangular shape of the window, and look very attractive.

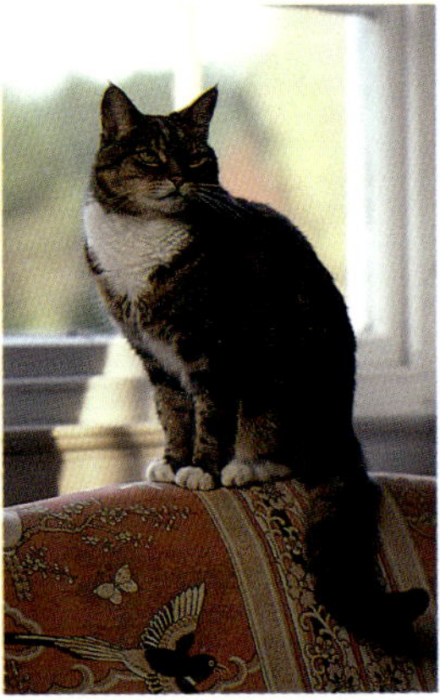

Set up the camera facing the window, and you can create backlighting, as described on page 53. Unless you are deliberately trying to create a silhouette, though, you must use a reflector or fit a flash to provide fill-in light.

Sunlit windows produce very high contrast lighting, and while the window is in sun, it is best to diffuse the light. Do this by covering the pane with net curtain, or tracing paper.

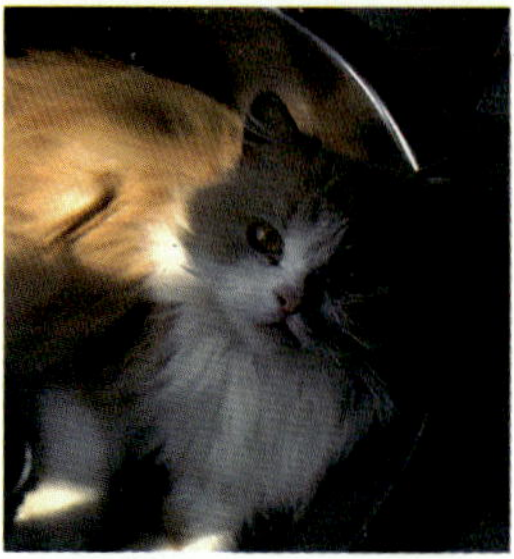

In the Sun ▲
If sun streams in, you'll get best results when the cat's face is in the shade.

Room Lights
If you have an adjustable camera, you can take advantage of whatever lights you have around the house. Use fast films such as KODACOLOR VR 400 and VR 1000 Films. These are specially made to give better colors than normal daylight films when used with tungsten and fluorescent light. Take off lamp shades, as these cut down the amount of light available, and move the cat as close to the lamp as it will go. Take care, though, as bulbs get very hot. Use the camera's meter in the normal way, making sure that you don't include the bulb in the viewfinder. Set the lens to a large aperture (low number) to gather as much light as possible. If the shutter speed falls below 1/60, provide extra camera support by resting your elbows on a table or chair, or by using a tripod.

Pictures taken by tungsten light with daylight film may seem too orangish. You can greatly reduce this tint by using a deep blue 80A filter over the camera lens (see page 59). The disadvantage of this approach is that the filter absorbs a lot of light, and may force you to use a shutter speed that is too slow for handholding of the camera.

Fluorescent tubes produce light that is deficient in red, leaving your pictures a bit too green. A special filter, called an FLD filter, eliminates this green tinge, and hardly absorbs any light.

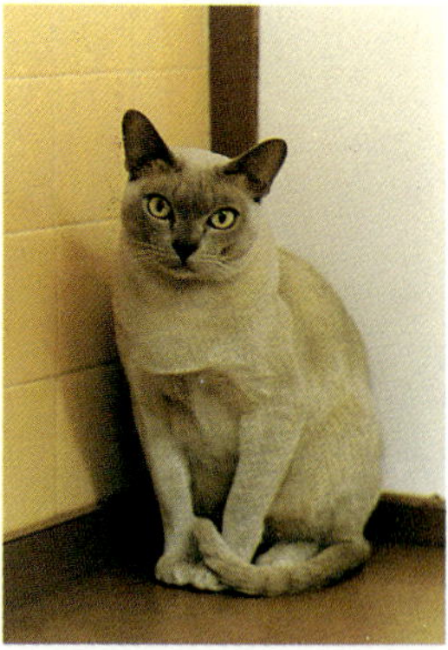

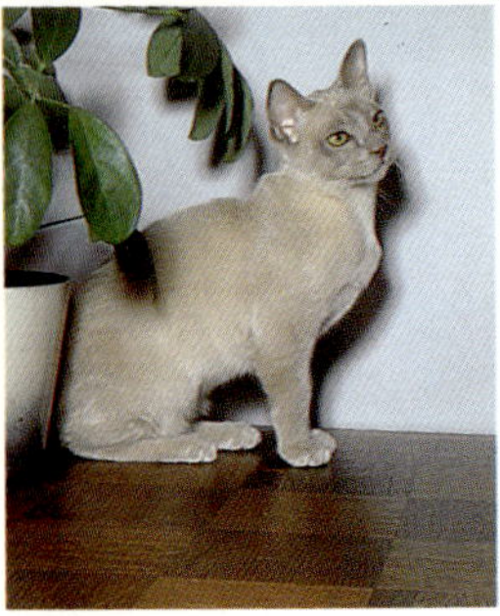

DIRECT FLASH

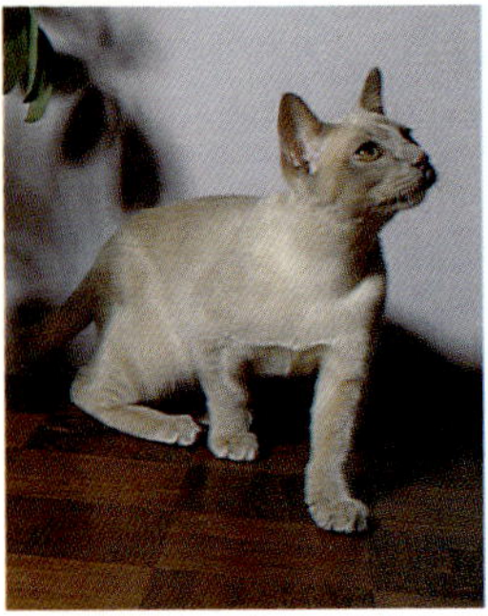

FLASH OFF CAMERA

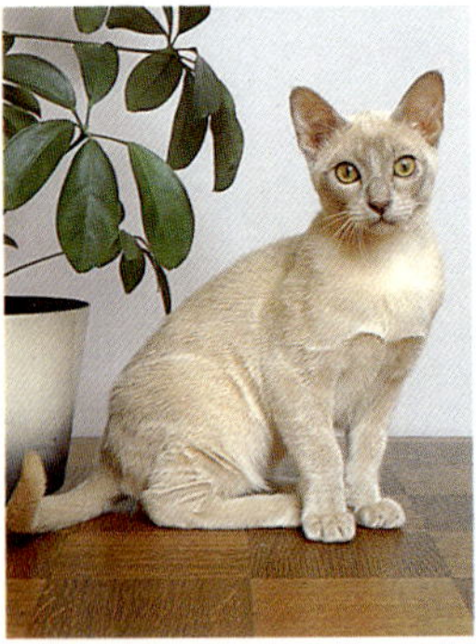

BOUNCE FLASH ▲ ▶

Better Flash Pictures

Most flash units have small reflectors that create harsh, flat lighting. Unfortunately there is little you can do about this if you have a very simple camera. However, if you can separate the flash from the camera, there are a couple of useful ways to improve how your cat is lit.

The first is to use an inexpensive extension cable to connect the camera to the flash, moving the flash unit out of the camera's hot shoe and well to one side of the cat. This makes the flash less frontal, and casts the cat's shadow sideways, instead of directly behind it. If you have a dedicated flash unit (see page 26) you may have to buy a special flash lead.

Bounce flash makes the lighting even softer and more attractive, but is only practical if your flash unit has a tilt head. With the unit mounted on the camera, angle the head at the ceiling or at a piece of white card held above the camera so that the light will bounce off the

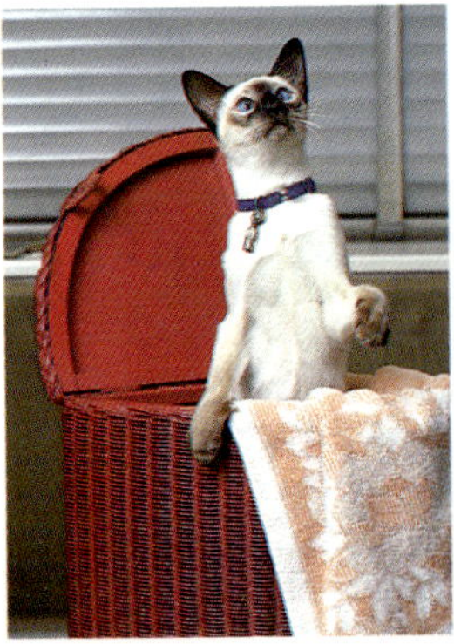

ceiling or card and onto the cat. By reflecting the beam you diffuse it, creating a more attractive lighting effect. Choose a wide aperture, and ensure that the distance the light from the flash travels (from flash to ceiling to cat) is no more than half the distance indicated on the calculator dial. Never bounce light from colored ceilings—this will tint the cat unnatural hues.

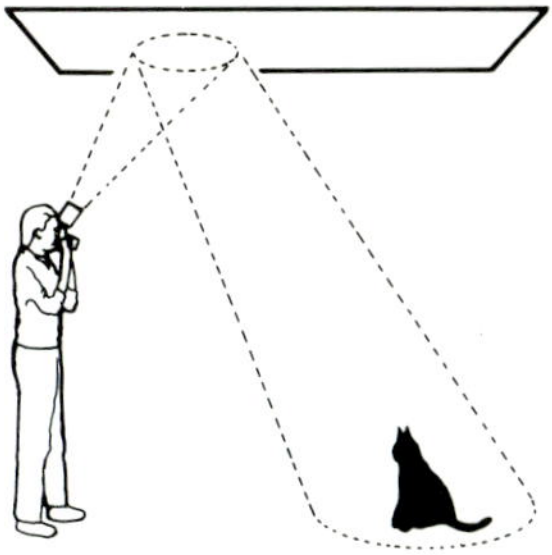

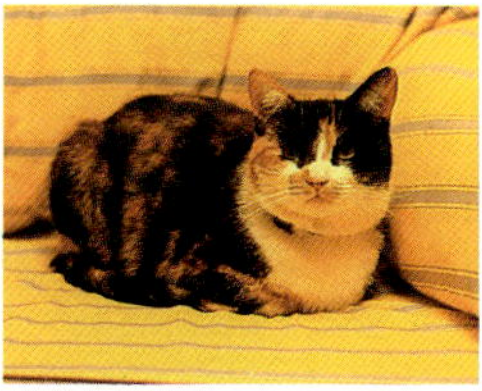

WITHOUT FILTER

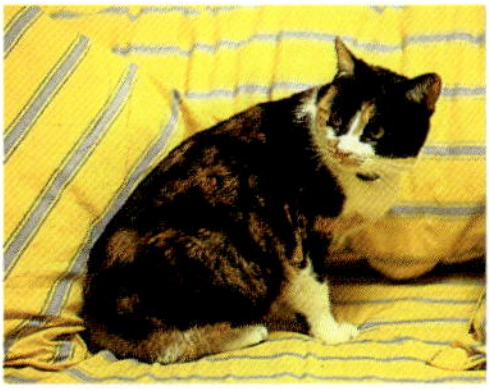

WITH BLUE 80A FILTER

Slide Film and Filters

Slide film is not nearly as tolerant of different light sources as negative film, and to get good results indoors, you may have to use colored filters over the lens. Light bulbs in particular cause problems, turning pictures taken by their light a strong orange color. You can cure this by fitting an 80A filter, but if you plan to take a lot of pictures using light bulbs, you should not buy ordinary daylight balanced slide film. Instead get tungsten-light-balanced film such as KODAK EKTACHROME 160

Light source	Daylight films such as KODAK EKTACHROME 100, 200 and 400, and KODACHROME 25 and 64 Films	Tungsten films such as KODAK EKTACHROME 160 and KODACHROME 40 Films
Window light	no filter	85B filter
Flash	no filter	85B filter
Tungsten light bulbs	80A filter	no filter
Fluorescent tubes	FLD filter	FLT filter

CATS TOGETHER

Keeping one frisky cat in front of the camera sometimes seems like an impossible task, and two cats can mean double the trouble. However, the rewards often more than balance the problems—as with human subjects, cats in pairs have each other to concentrate on, and are more inclined to forget the camera.

Cats that live together usually eat from the same bowl, wash each other, and sleep curled up together in a confusion of furry limbs. When you unite them in front of the camera they will show typical social behavior, rubbing their backs together and sniffing each other. Unless the cats have been apart for several days, though, they won't usually make a great show of affection—so there's no point in locking them in separate rooms prior to taking pictures. However, if one of them has been away for a while, they may make more of their meeting, and inspect each other with greater thoroughness, and this is sure to be worth a picture.

Bringing together in front of the camera two cats that are strangers is a different matter altogether—you'll almost certainly arouse territorial instincts, and if you're not careful, you'll have a cat fight on your hands. Cats are by nature solitary, independent creatures, and don't take kindly to unwanted introductions. There is, however, one useful trick that you might try: cats identify each other largely on the basis of smell, and if you make the two animals smell the same, they will settle down together more quickly. Do this by spraying each with perfume (be careful to avoid their eyes) or by smearing each with sardine oil.

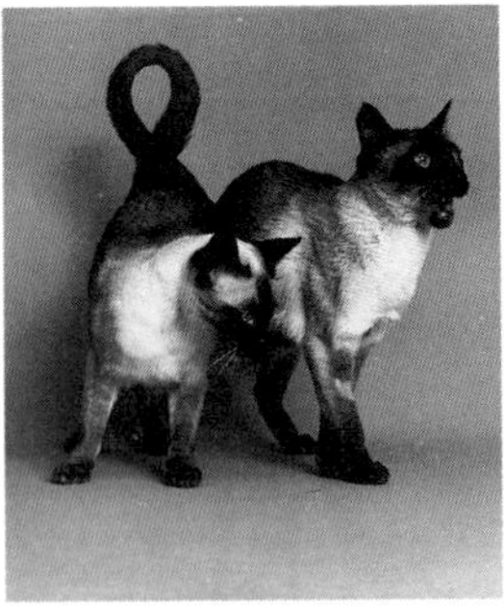

◀ **Motion and Shutter Speed**
If the two cats move around a lot, you may want to set a fast shutter speed to freeze them on film. Again, bright light and fast film help, but usually you'll find that you can't set both a fast speed and a small aperture. If you face this problem, try using flash to arrest the cats' antics, as explained on page 91.

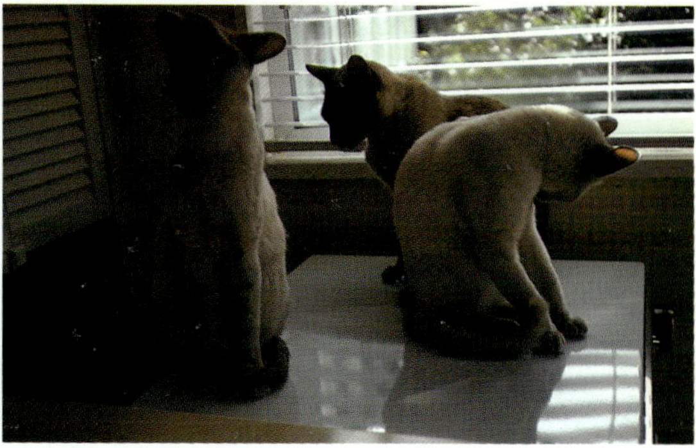

Framing and Focusing ▲

Cats in pairs make good subjects for simple cameras, because you can get better pictures from a greater distance. Whatever kind of camera you have, allow your cats plenty of room in the frame, as they will probably move around a lot more than when you picture them singly. The problems that depth of field creates with one cat are increased with two. You can turn a single cat sideways so as to reduce its depth, but the only way to keep two cats sharp is to set a small aperture. If your camera does not have manual control over aperture, either use a faster film or take pictures in bright light—both these steps force many automatic cameras to set a smaller aperture.

In a Row ▼

If your cats are docile enough, arrange them in a row at equal distances from the camera, to minimize depth of field problems.

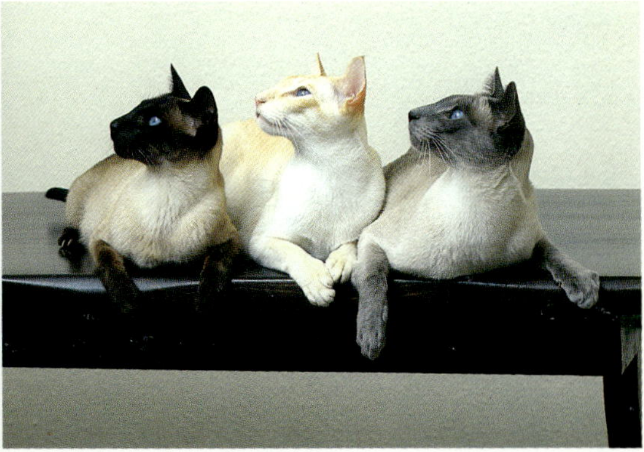

Keeping Control

You can use many of the techniques described on pages 42-3 to keep your cats under control, but it is important to remember that an excitable cat is liable to become almost uncontrollable when there are other cats around, so any problems that you had in photographing the cat alone are liable to be aggravated. Warmth, though, is still a great persuader, particularly with shorter-haired breeds. Keep the room in which you are taking pictures fairly cool, and the cats will gravitate towards any hot spot out of the drafts. Bear in mind, though, that heat can be very soporific, and you'll need to use another trick to get the attention of the cats, if you don't want a picture of them sleeping. Use noise, movement and toys to attract their gaze.

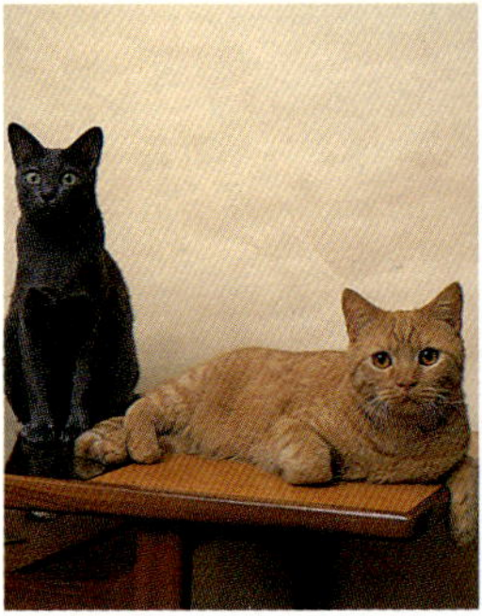

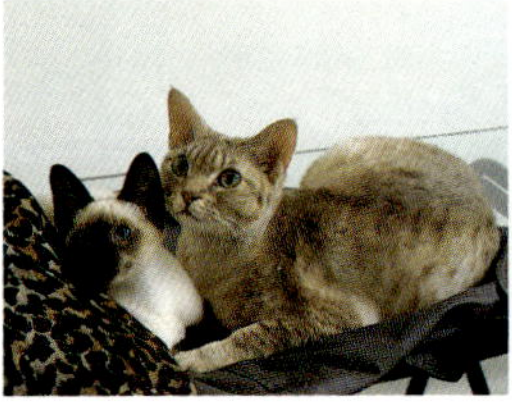

A Shared Meal

Food is as valuable an aid with two cats as with one, and you'll find that butter in particular will induce the pair to wash each other.

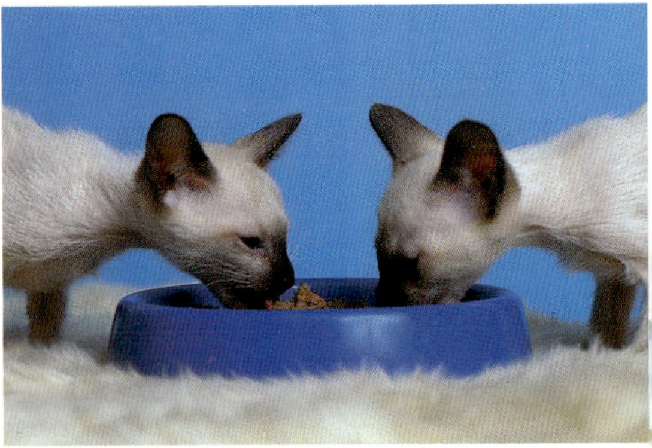

Extra Hands

Never try to hold down two cats that refuse to be photographed together, or you will risk an unpleasant scratch or bite. A little help, though, is useful when the cats are merely excitable, not aggressive. Ideally, enlist two helpers, one to hold each cat firmly but gently, and to stroke and comfort it while you focus and compose the picture. When you're about to take the picture, tell your helpers to release their charges. Take pictures quickly, as you are likely to have only a couple of seconds available before the cats tear off in different directions.

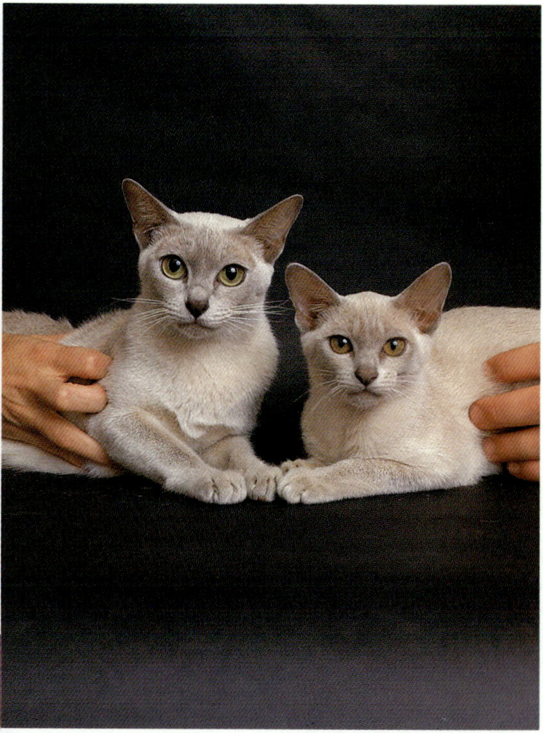

Skittish Subjects

Use helpers to keep reluctant cats still — you can crop their hands out of the final print.

PHOTOGRAPHING KITTENS

Like most small mammals, kittens are wonderfully amusing little creatures, and their tricks and games are particularly photogenic—if you are quick enough to catch them. In the years to come, the pictures you take of a kitten will provide a lasting reminder that your proudly strutting tomcat was once a helpless little bundle of fluff.

For the first few weeks of life, though, kittens do not look particularly pretty. Their eyes are closed until they are about ten days old, and the mother will usually prefer to keep them in a dark, well-protected spot far from the prying eye of a camera. After about six weeks, kittens look more like real cats, albeit in miniature: their ears are straighter and more upright, their coats are smoother, and they look generally less scraggy. From this point on, kittens grow rapidly, so don't stint on film—pictures taken just a week apart will show visible differences.

Simple Camera Close-Ups ▼
If you have a simple camera then you'll probably have most success if you photograph several kittens in one picture, taking care to ensure that you don't get nearer than your camera's closest focusing distance. To be on the safe side, measure out the minimum focusing distance given in your camera's instruction book, and mark two lines on the ground exactly this distance apart as the photographer did for this picture. Then make sure that neither you nor the kittens stray into the space between the lines.

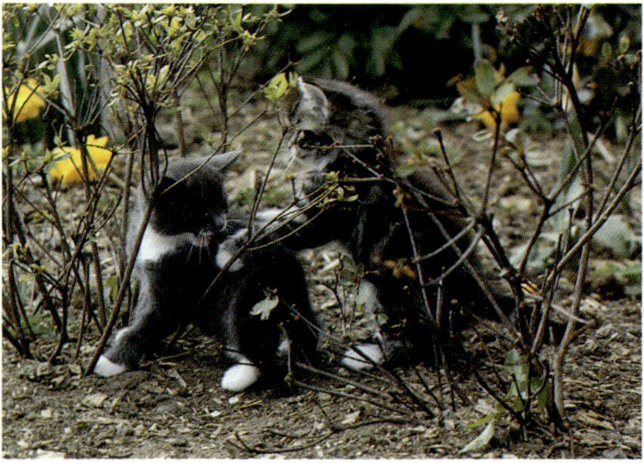

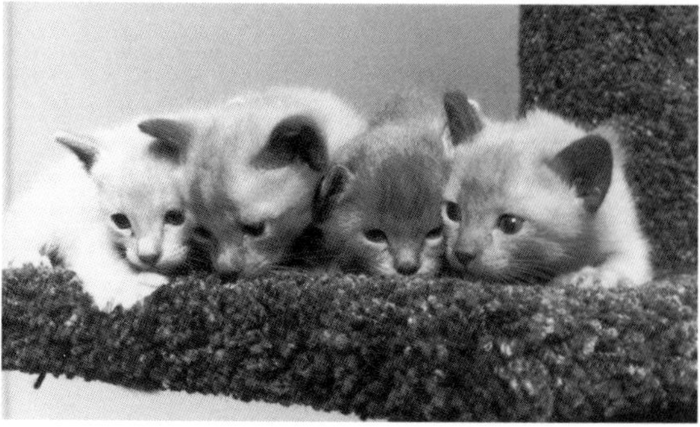

Keeping Kittens in Focus ▲

The closer together you move subject and camera, the shallower is the zone of sharp focus, and the more accurate focusing must be to produce consistently sharp pictures. If a kitten is just inches from the lens, the only way to be sure that it will be sharp on film is to use an SLR camera with a close-up accessory such as an extension tube or a supplementary close-up lens (see page 23).

Even with the right equipment, you may find it hard to focus. Instead of turning the focusing ring to do this, try leaving it on a single setting, and move the camera back and forth. Press the shutter release as soon as the kitten's eyes are sharp in the viewfinder.

At really close distances, you'll be lucky to get the whole kitten sharp, but stopping the aperture down as small as the light permits will maximize the depth of field. Use the SLR camera's depth-of-field preview control to see how much is sharp.

If dim light prevents you from setting a small aperture, try using flash, but be aware that this may in turn introduce exposure problems. With the exception of supplementary lenses, all close-up accessories absorb light. Normally your camera's TTL meter compensates for the light lost, but this does not happen when you use flash. To avoid underexposure with color negative film, give one stop extra exposure. With slide film, consult the instructions packed with the close-up accessory.

Restricting Movement ▼

Kittens can't balance well, so use only quite low platforms to confine them.

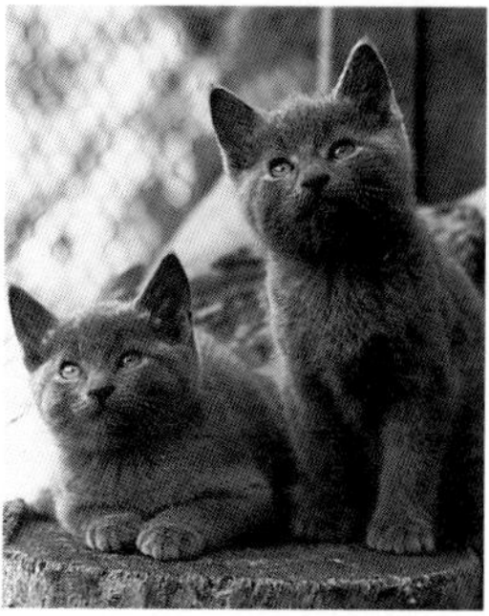

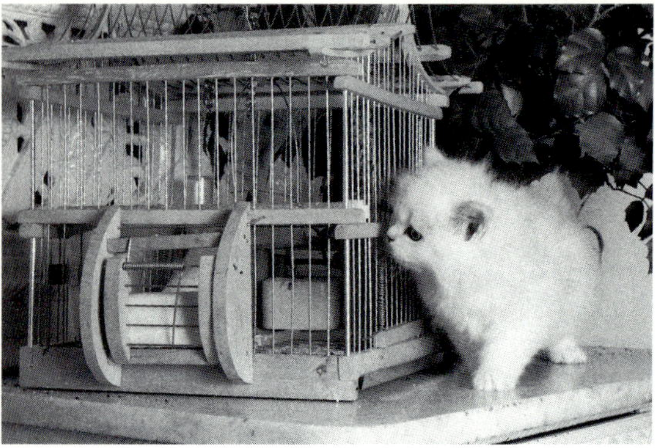

First Encounters

As soon as kittens are up and walking, they explore their new world. This gives the photographer a once-only opportunity to take pictures of the kittens discovering each new object and experience for the first time. Be ready with a camera as they first encounter a bird or another animal besides a cat. Take them out into the garden, and photograph them as they first smell a flower. Sit them in front of the TV and watch their wide-eyed astonishment. See what happens when a kitten first spots its own reflection in a mirror.

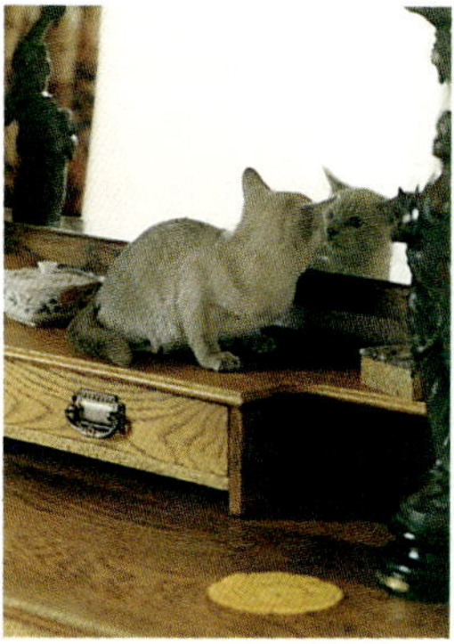

Most important of all, though, make sure that you have plenty of film, and a camera at the ready. Set the controls either to flash (but see opposite) or to the prevailing light.

Size and Scale ▶

Look for settings that emphasize a kitten's tiny proportions.

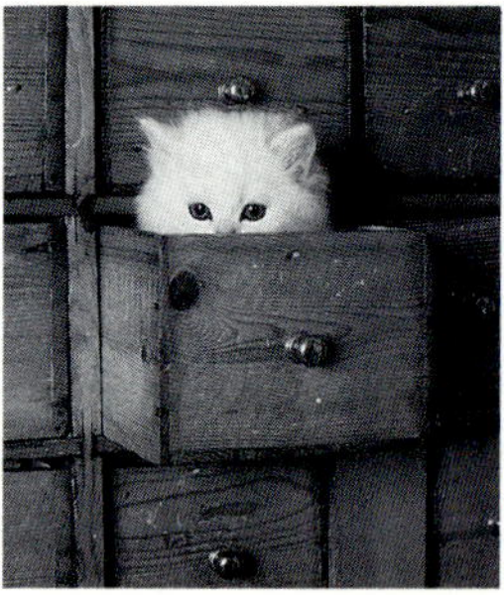

Close Up Flash ▶

Many people worry that the burst of light from a flash unit will harm the delicate newly-open eyes of a kitten, but these fears are unfounded. After an initial start, kittens will barely notice the flash.

However, if you get your camera and flash really close to a kitten—and to fill the frame, you'll have to—you may occasionally find that the flash unit does not function normally, and your pictures are overexposed. If you encounter this problem,

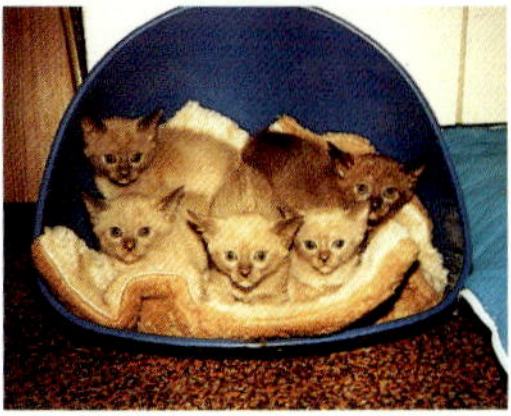

close down the camera's aperture or with a non-adjustable camera, tape tracing paper or white tissue over the reflector. Or try bouncing the flash light from a piece of white card as explained on page 59.

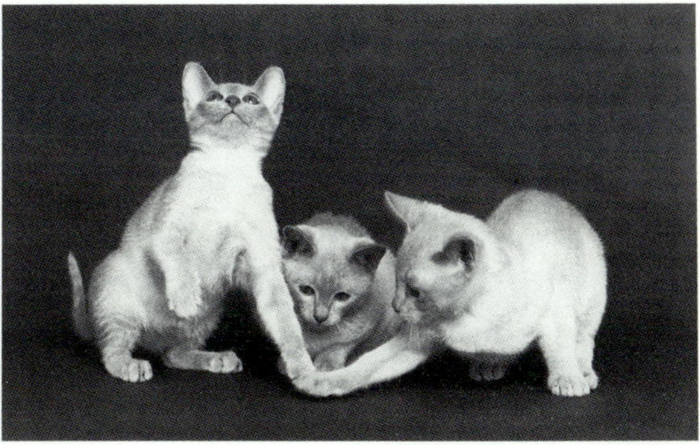

Kitten Care

Until it has been innoculated at the age of 10-12 weeks, a kitten is very vulnerable to disease, so don't try to photograph it with any cats other than the mother, or its brothers and sisters from the same litter. Young cats' bones are soft, so kittens should always be handled with the greatest of care. Never pick them up by the scruff of the neck—always cradle them in your hand.

Flash and Movement ▲

The action-stopping power of flash has special value with frisky kittens.

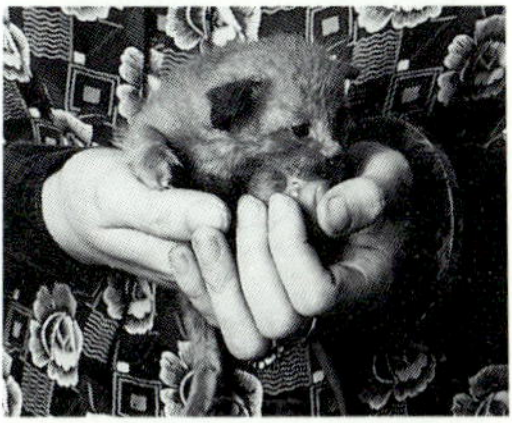

MOTHER CAT AND KITTENS

Portraits of families always make attractive pictures and never more so than when the family is a furry feline one. A cat makes the most devoted and attentive of mothers, and long before the birth she will be busy preparing for the new family. Unfortunately, photographic recording of her kittens' first minutes will not be her first priority, and you can be sure that the birth will take place in the most innaccessible and inconvenient of places, such as the very back of your darkest closet!

Nesting in such secluded spots is a throwback to the cat's undomesticated past, and it is only fair to respect this desire for privacy. You should therefore think twice before attempting to photograph the birth itself. Even if it is your own cat she may be disturbed by your presence when the kittens are due, and if there are any signs of this, leave her completely alone until the litter is a few hours old.

Family Snapshots

For the first few weeks of life, kittens stay very close to the mother, doing little more than sleeping and feeding. Arranging a picture of the family at this stage is one of the few instances where a cat's-eye-level view does not produce a better picture. Instead of getting down to ground level, stand over the mother cat as her kittens suckle, and make the most of the pattern of tiny forms enclosed and protected by her legs.

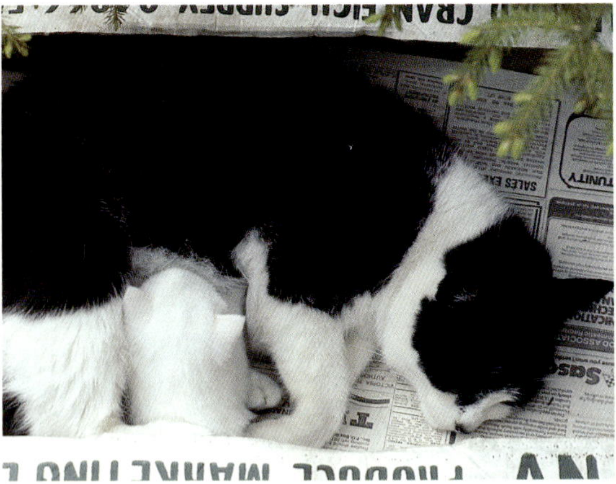

Natural Light or Flash?

As explained on the previous page, flash does no harm to cat or kittens, and is a perfectly satisfactory way of making a straightforward record of mother and family. However, you may prefer the softer, more sympathetic rendering produced by available light.

Move whatever lights you have quite close to the cat and kittens, and put pieces of white card on the far side to soften shadows. Then take pictures using fast film such as KODACOLOR VR 1000 film.

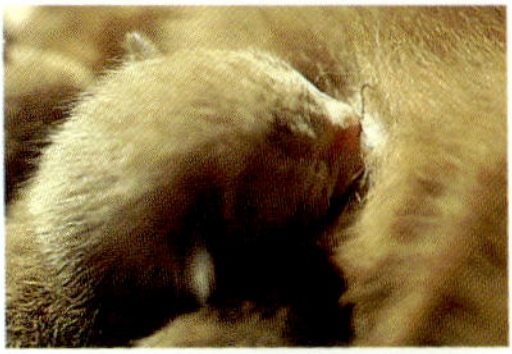

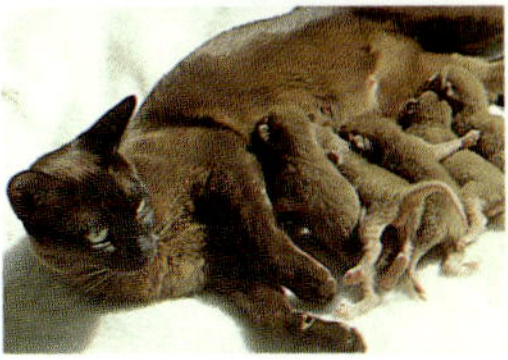

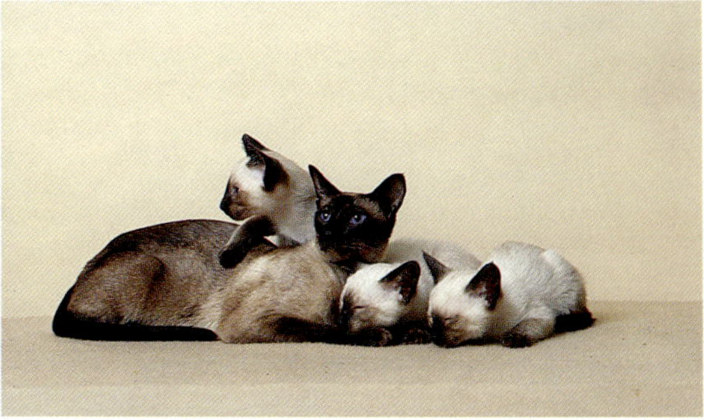

Alert Expressions

Kittens and mother sleep very soundly, and you can use this knowledge to advantage. Have a warm place ready, using a heating pad or a couple of hot water bottles, and cover it with a soft, cozy material such as fur fabric. Let the kittens exhaust themselves from play, and wait until they curl up for a doze with mom. While they are sleeping soundly, you can gently move them round the heated area to make a more pleasing composition. When everything is arranged, make a loud noise—perhaps by clapping your hands—and cat and kittens will all wake up and look for the source of the noise. You will have to be very quick to catch their looks of surprise with your camera, because the kittens will all shoot off in different directions, and it will take them time to settle down again. Don't repeat the procedure too often, either, or you could soon become unpopular with the mother!

YOUR CAT'S WORLD

Like posed photos of people, feline portraits show subjects on their best behavior, groomed and neat for the camera. The emphasis is on flattery, on getting a good likeness—perhaps on showing off your pedigree cat's aristocratic profile to best effect!

However, as any owner knows, cats can be willfull and impatient. No sooner have you turned your back to load film, than your carefully-combed long-hair is darting out to roll in the nearest pile of grass-cuttings, or sharpening its claws on an armchair.

In all fairness to the cat, though, this independence is what makes it appealing: people who like pets to be constantly at their beck and call usually buy dogs or goldfish. If your cat won't pose for a portrait, perhaps you should try a more naturalistic approach, taking candid pictures of your cat as it goes about its day-to-day business.

This type of photography doesn't require the same skills as portrait photography. Instead you'll have to learn the cunning of the paparazzi, who follows an unwilling celebrity in the hope of a picture. And you'll need to develop the patience of a wildlife photographer, who sits in a hide on a game reserve, waiting for a glimpse of a (bigger) cat.

Feline High Rise

A cats world stretches out in all directions, even (or especially) upwards. To catch these urban cats patrolling the rooftops, the photographer used a telephoto lens. The white wall misled the camera's meter, so she set exposure to manual and took a meter reading from a shaded area instead.

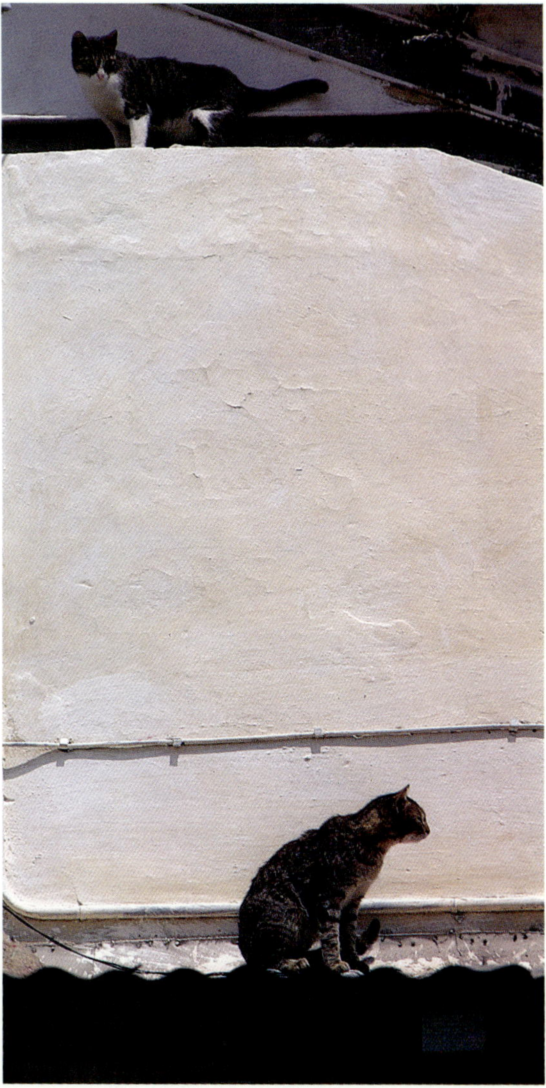

STARTING OUTDOORS

Many cat-owners have little idea what their pet gets in to when the kitchen door closes or the cat-flap slams shut. The exception of course is when squeals in the night and a torn ear in the morning give the game away. So before picking up a camera, it may be worthwhile doing a little domestic natural history, and finding out exactly how your cat spends its time.

You can get a hint of this by watching it while you sit in the sun on a patch of grass, but even then, your cat's behavior is likely to be largely conditioned by your presence. To get pictures of what a cat really gets in to, you'll have to make sure it doesn't see you.

Catching a Glimpse
Try keeping an eye on your cat from an upper floor window. You'll have a good view of the area around your house, and you'll soon be able to pick out a number of likely vantage points from which to take pictures. You may even find that the window itself provides a suitable camera position, provided you can fit a telephoto lens to your camera (see page 78).

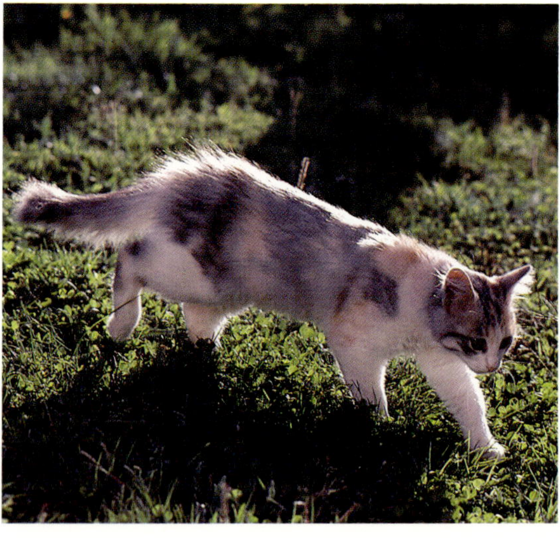

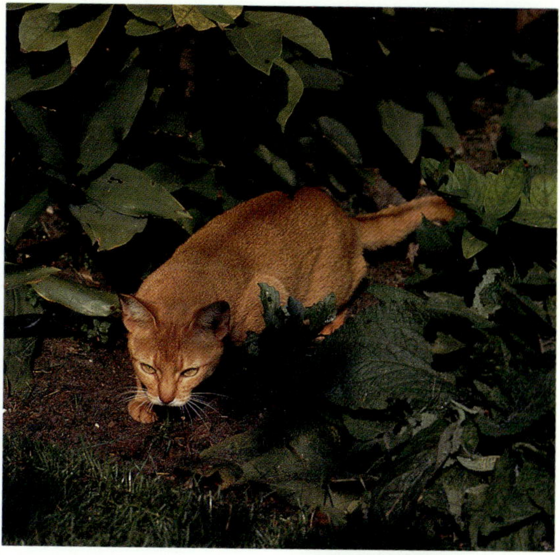

Stalking Your Pet

A camouflaged photographer stalking a cat around suburban streets is a ridiculous idea worthy of a Marx Brothers film. Nevertheless, the simpler skills of the wildlife photographer can be usefully adapted to the photography of domesticated subjects—though without the blackened face and battle fatigues!

If you are trying to take pictures unobserved, you'll want to make as little noise as possible. Wear sneakers, rather than hard-soled shoes, and make sure that you have on soft clothing that doesn't rustle as you move.

A cat's eyesight perceives movement very clearly, but static shapes hardly at all. So keep still if your cat looks straight at you, and move only when it is distracted by something else. Silhouettes against the sky are particularly visible, especially to a cat at ground level. This doesn't mean you have to wriggle on your belly—just use a bit of common sense, such as not crossing streets with the sun behind you.

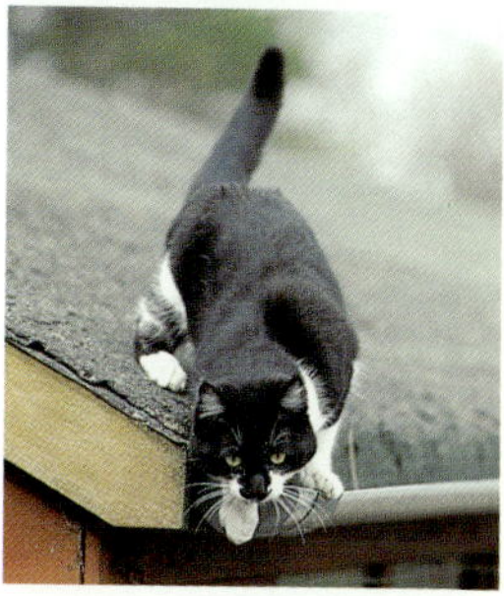

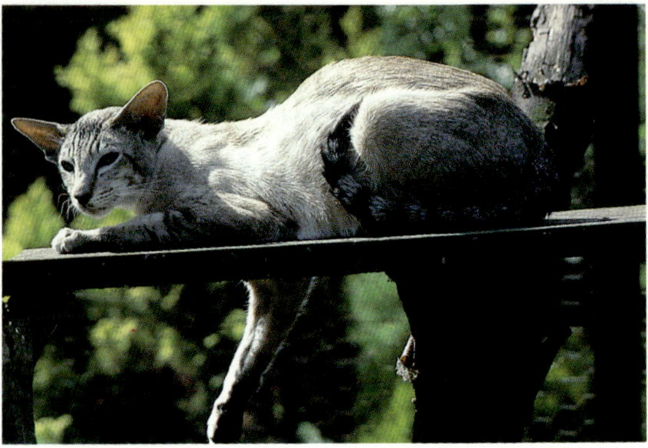

Dawn and Dusk

Much feline activity takes place at night, and you'll be able to catch such escapades only if you use flash. However, in the fading light of dusk and in the early morning, fast film such as KODACOLOR VR 1000 Film will make better use of what light there is.

EKTACHROME 400 Film is a good transparency film for dim light. It can be used at its normal speed of ISO 400 or its speed can be doubled to ISO 800 if given extended processing. If you are doubling the speed, shoot the whole roll at ISO 800, and buy from your photo dealer a KODAK Special Processing Envelope, ESP-1.

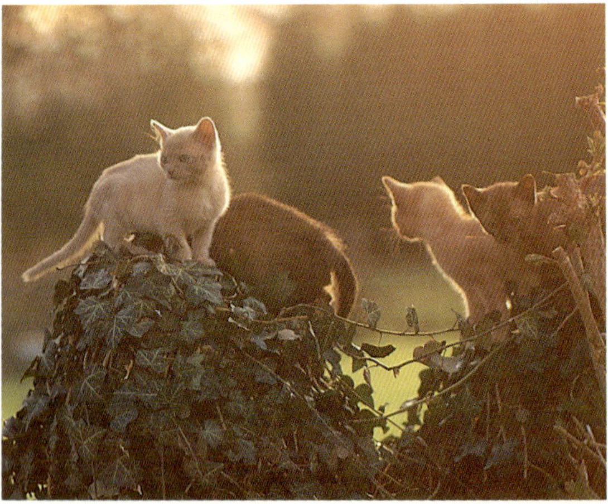

A Story in Pictures

If you've tracked your cat like a photojournalist, why not present the pictures in an appropriate way? You may find that you have an interesting sequence of images that makes up a brief narrative—a feline picture-story. Try mounting or framing them together to highlight your cat's travels and adventures around the neighborhood.

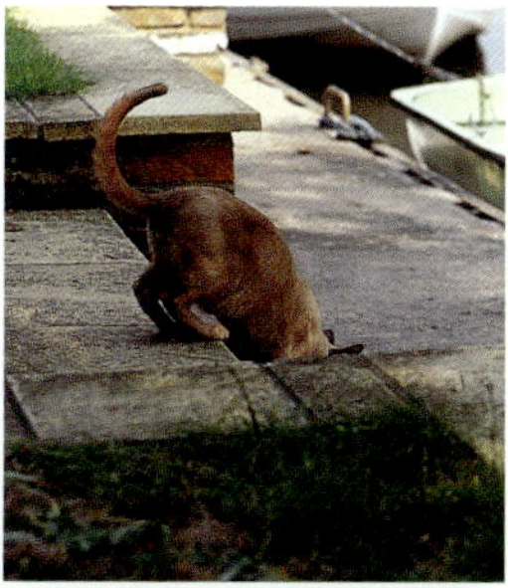

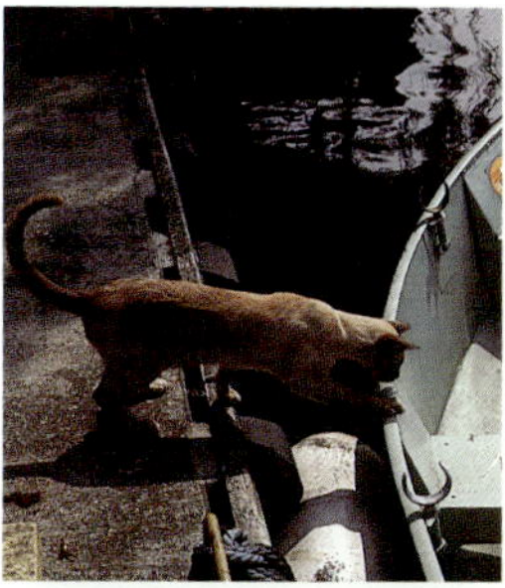

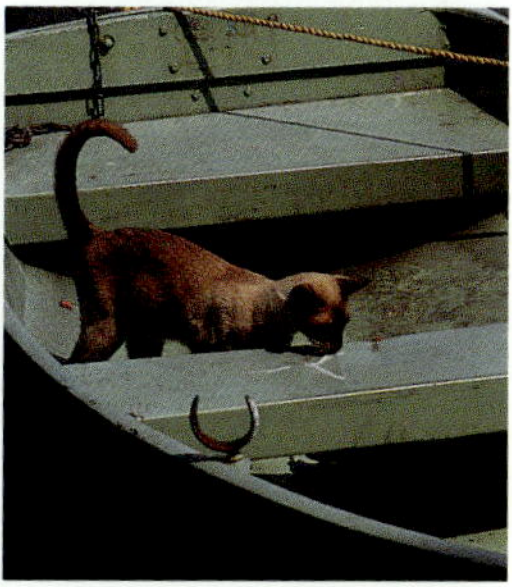

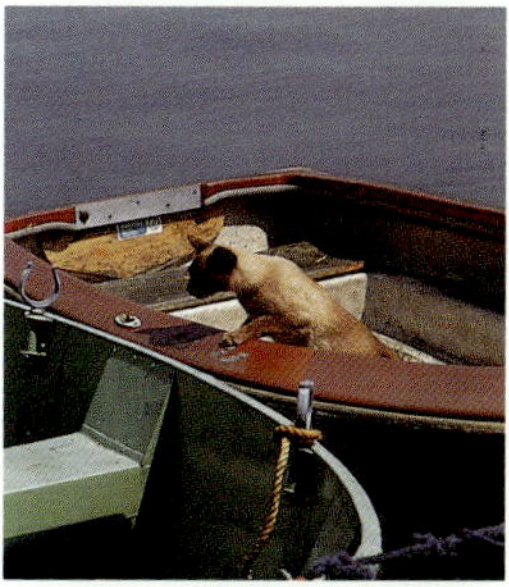

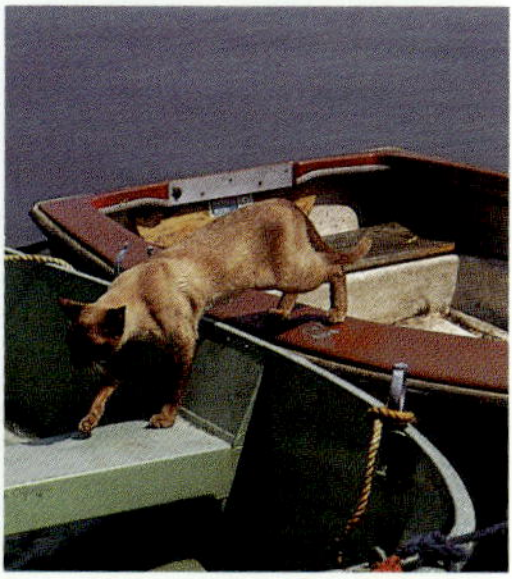

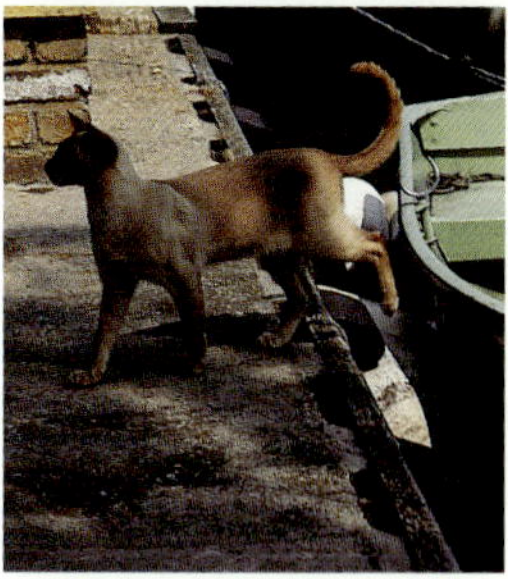

PICKING GOOD VIEWPOINTS

Being a small creature, your cat sees things from a much lower viewpoint than you, and if you want pictures that show the world from a feline point of view, you'll have to get down to the cat's level.

This usually means crawling around on your hands and knees to get the most natural angle—not the most elegant of poses, and not to be recommended if you are wearing clothes that show the dirt. So if you plan to take cat-level pictures out of doors, wear the clothes you normally reserve for gardening or working on the family auto. Cats may pose at a height closer to a human viewpoint, such as on a fence or wall, but most of the time you'll find that they're on the ground, and you must be prepared to get down to it on their level.

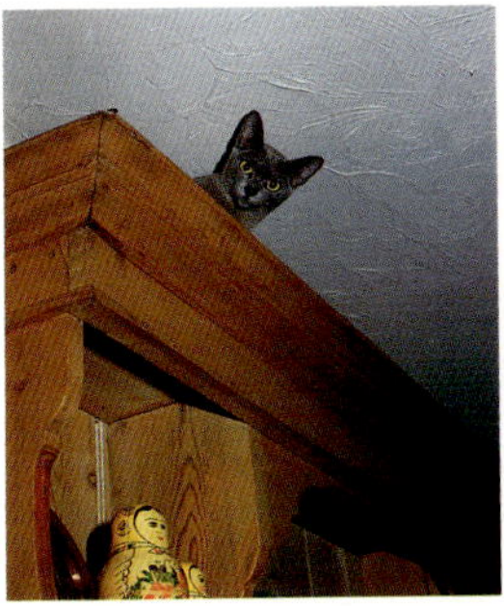

Indoors
In the home, a low viewpoint is less uncomfortable, and you'll find the cat on other levels, too—some of which don't even demand a floor-level camera. Cats like to roost in high places such as on top of the freezer or TV (both are warm spots) or on bookshelves, mantlepieces or pianos. To get a natural looking, cat's-eye perspective of these spots, you'll need to stand on a chair or stool, to raise yourself off the ground. Try a few pictures from lower down, too, pointing the camera steeply upwards. The resulting pictures will have a dizzying perspective that emphasizes the height of your cat's aerie.

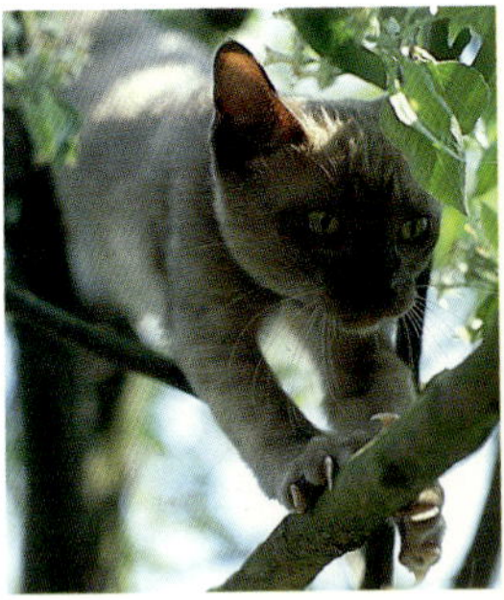

Sharpening Claws
Trees not only keep cats relatively still, they also provide the photographer with effortless eye-level views.

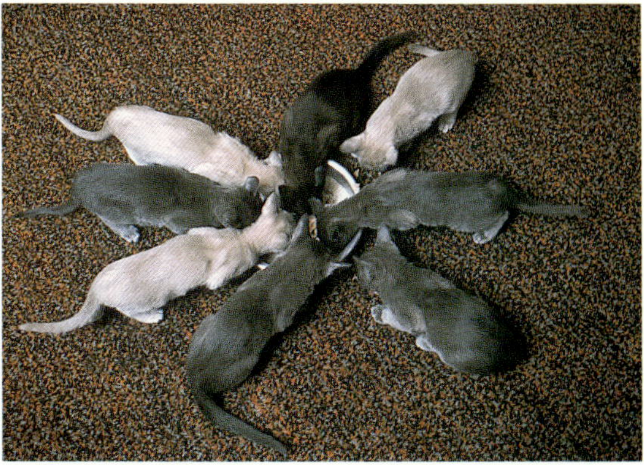

Look Down For Pattern

Occasionally you can use your height to advantage to make attractive feline patterns. For this picture, the photographer pointed the camera directly down towards a circle of kittens around a bowl.

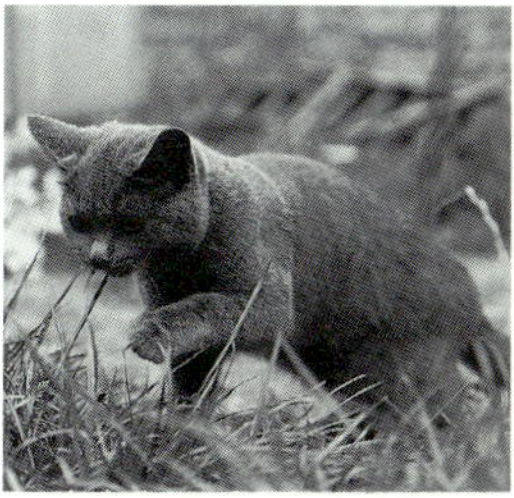

Cameras For Low Views

If you want to avoid sprawling on the ground for a low viewpoint, just fit a wide-angle lens to your camera, and guess the framing and focusing. Wide-angle lenses provide ample leeway for errors in both areas.

If you have a simpler camera, you might try the same technique—most of these cameras have moderately wide-angle lenses, too.

Twin-lens-reflex cameras are often available at knock-down prices, and have a viewfinder that you can look down into, as at right. These cameras give you a naturally lower viewpoint, and you can easily rest them on the floor for pictures literally at ground level.

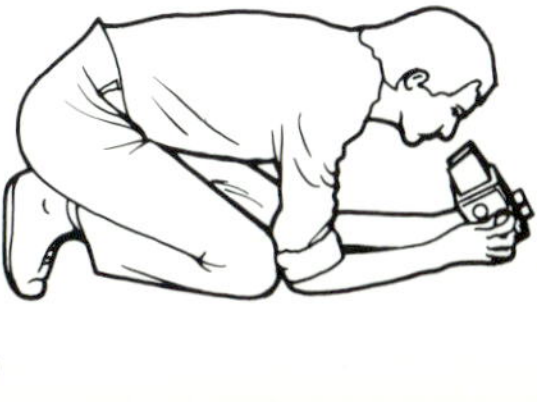

KEEPING YOUR DISTANCE

If you have an SLR, you'll find that fitting a telephoto lens enables you to get good pictures of your cat from a greater distance. In the garden, a telephoto lens allows you to pick out your cat foraging in flower beds, or perched on the fence—all without it being aware of the camera or photographer.

People who are used to looking through binoculars and telescopes are often surprised at how little a telephoto lens magnifies the cat: the most popular lenses enlarge the image only three to five times. This is enough, though, to make a big difference to your pictures.

The focal length of the lens gives a guide to its magnification. For example, a 200 mm lens has a focal length four times longer than your camera's normal lens, and therefore makes a four times bigger image of the cat. Other popular focal lengths are 135 mm, and 105 mm. Shorter focal lengths provide too little magnification to be useful, and lenses longer than 200 mm tend to be heavy, expensive and difficult to use.

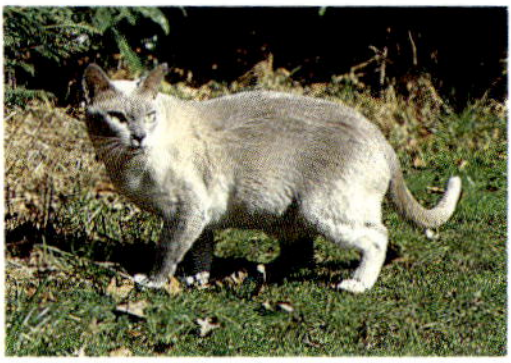

100 mm LENS

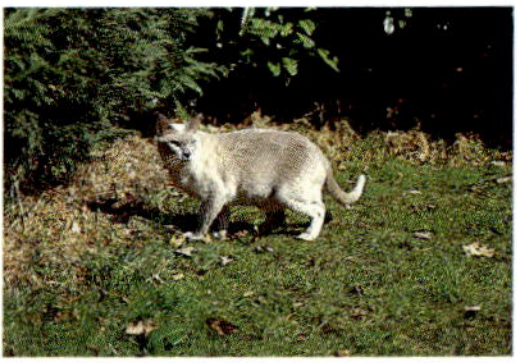

NORMAL LENS

Zoom Lenses

Some lenses provide a continuously variable range of focal lengths. These zoom lenses let you fine-tune the composition of your picture to neatly frame the cat without moving the camera. They are great if you don't want to carry more than one lens, but they don't usually let as much light into the camera as fixed-focal-length lenses—so in dim light you'll have to use faster film or a slower shutter speed. Zoom lenses are also heavier and more costly than regular telephoto lenses.

Typical telephoto zoom lenses cover a focal length range of 70-210 mm, or 80-200 mm. Some go right down to normal lens length (50 mm) and a few to the wide-angle range—35 or 28 mm.

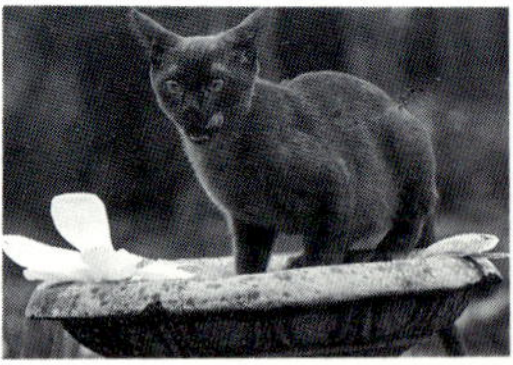

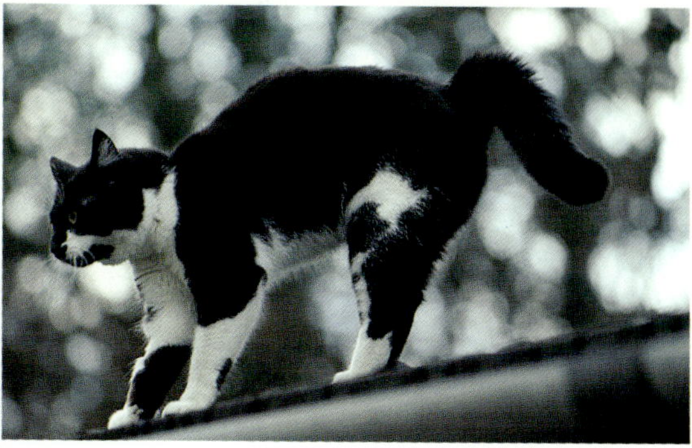

On the Prowl
Long lenses are especially useful when it is physically impossible to get closer to your pet.

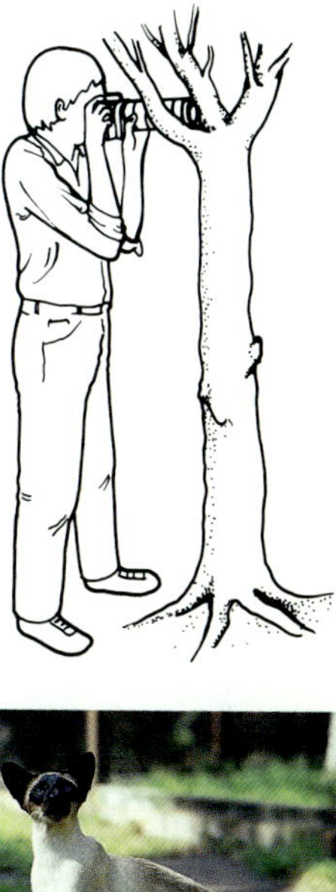

Use Extra Support
Besides magnifying the cat, a telephoto lens also exaggerates camera shake to the same degree so rest the lens on any convenient support, as at right. To keep your pictures sharp when handholding a telephoto, set a shutter speed roughly equal to the focal length. So for a 200 mm lens, use 1/250 second. A fast film such as KODACOLOR VR 400 Film will enable you to set these faster speeds in dim light.

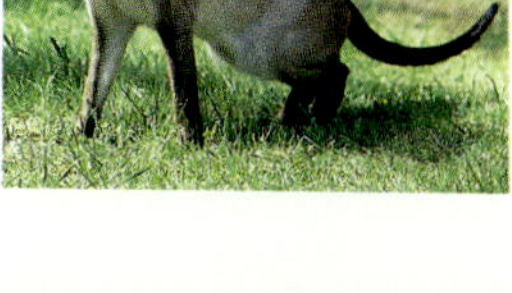

Depth of Field
Longer lenses keep less of your cat in focus, so that for nose-to-tail sharpness, you have to use smaller apertures. The reduced depth of field at normal apertures can be an advantage, though, when it blurs the background, making your cat's features stand out more clearly from the surroundings.

OTHER PEOPLE'S CATS

In the city and suburbs, there's hardly a patch of grass, or a square foot of tarmac that isn't staked out as the territory of one cat or another. A few of these street cats are unkempt feral cats, scratching an existence from garbage bins and terrorizing the local rodent population. But many are household pets that are sleek, well-fed, and photogenic. Breezing in to honor their owners with a brief visit at meal times and to sleep in the comfort of a house or apartment, they spend much of the rest of the day and night patrolling their patch.

All these cats are potential subjects for your camera. You can spot them and photograph them in environments where you'd fear for the safety of your own pet: silhouetted against the sky on the ridge of a roof, or prowling among the cranes at the local docks. To get great character pictures of these free spirits of the cat world, you'll need to carry your camera with you all the time. Leave it gathering dust in a cupboard and you will miss all the best pictures.

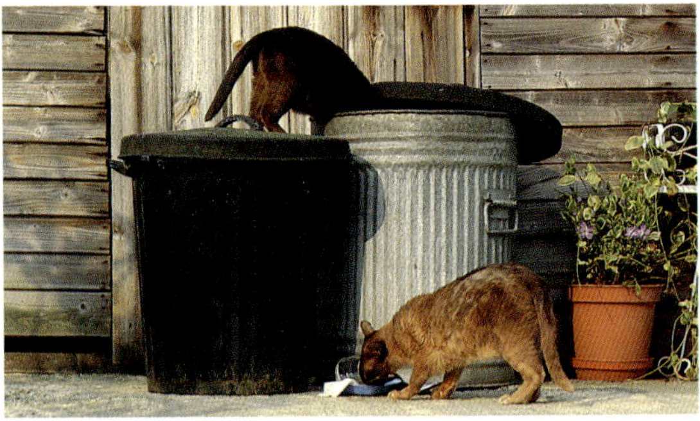

Show the Background
To bring out the difference between these alley cats and your favorite house-cat, try and catch them in surroundings that suggest their bohemian life-style. This is a rare instance where you might want to use a wide-angle lens to put the cat into context.

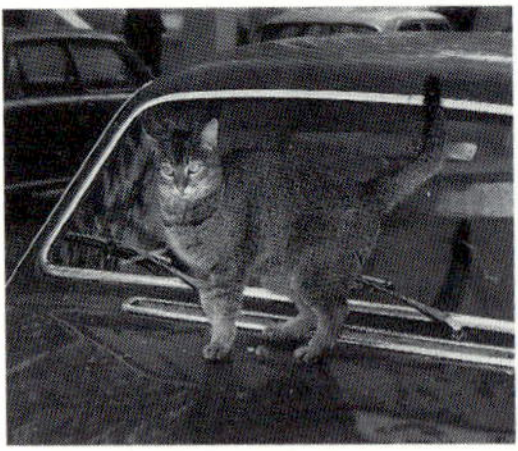

Working Cats

Many cats still "sing for their supper" by acting as a furry pest control operative. Visit small old-style shops for pictures like the one below—but take fast film or a flash to cope with the dark corners where cats often sit to survey their domain.

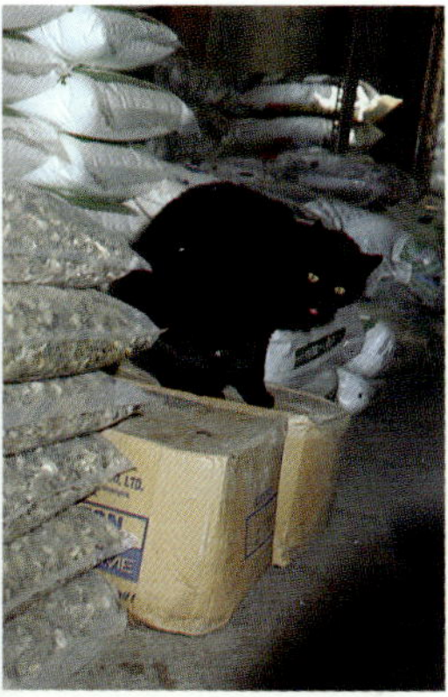

Balancing Act

Use a long lens to close in on delicately poised feline steeplejacks high above the ground.

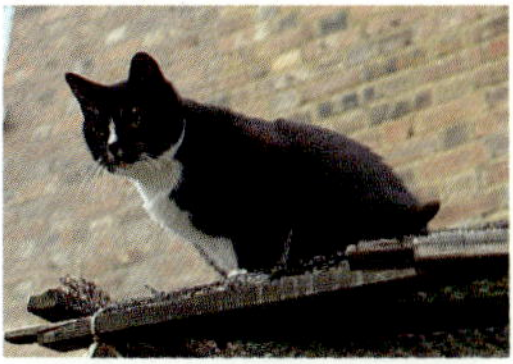

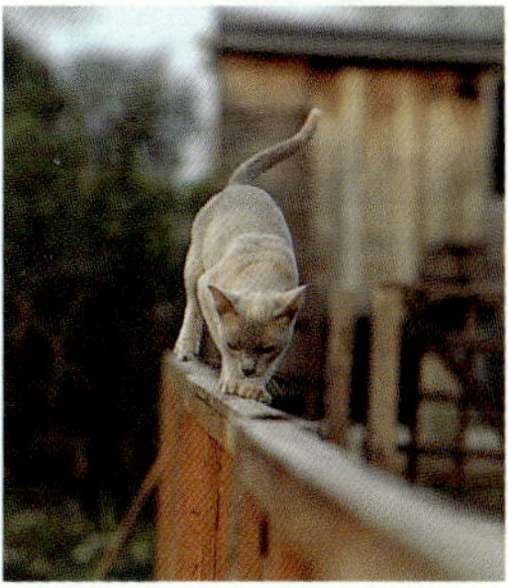

In a Scrap

If the fur flys, think twice before intervening: scratches and bites can easily become infected.

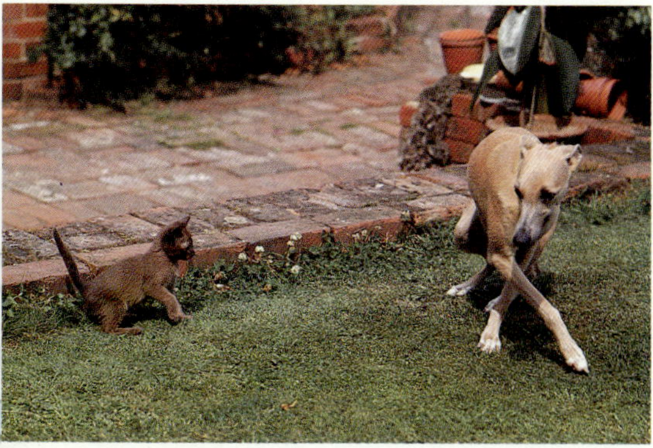

NATURAL VIEWS INDOORS

What do cats do indoors? Sleeping, washing, and eating are obvious activities that take up much of a cat's time, but each individual cat has its own individual tricks, habits and routines that you may want to picture on film. Some of their habits, such as opening the refrigerator door for a clandestine meal, will not endear the cat to its owner, but will make a good photo all the same!

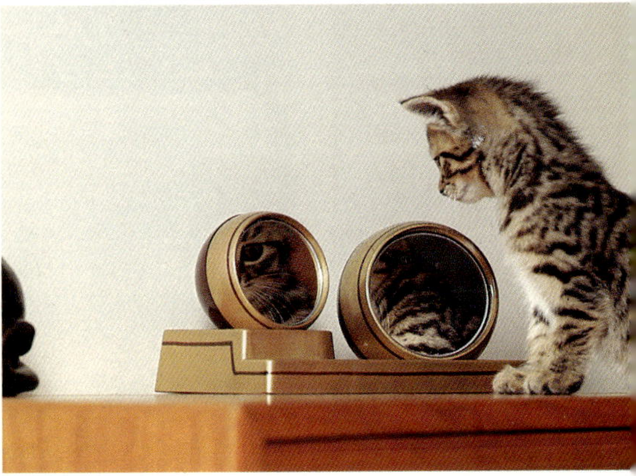

Be Prepared ▲

Keep a camera handy at all times, and make sure that it's set to auto and loaded with film. For grab-shots in the home, auto-focus cameras are ideal: you can reach out and pick up the camera, frame and click before the cat realizes that it's been caught in the act!

Lighting ▶

Unless you have a simple camera or one that gives you no manual control at all, try not to use direct on-camera flash for your "slice of life" cat pictures. Direct flash will give the pictures an artificial, staged look. Instead use bounce flash, as explained on page 59, or else load a fast film and take pictures by available light. If you decide not to use flash, maximize what light there is in simple ways: draw the drapes back as far as they will go, to let in as much daylight as possible. If your room lights are on dimmers, make sure that these are turned up to maximum power.

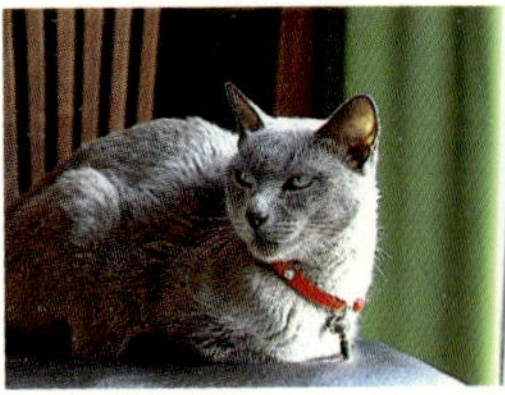

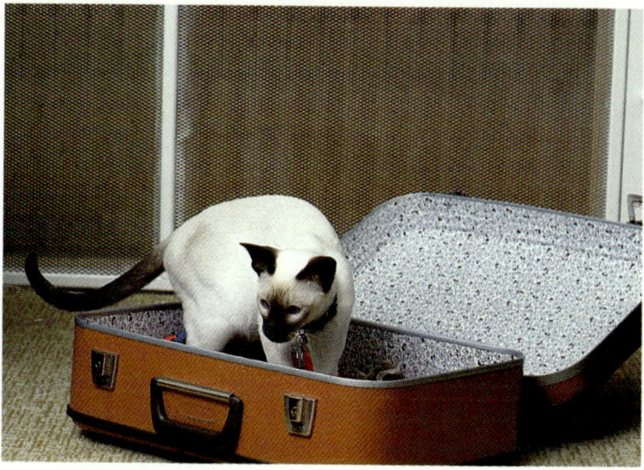

Take a Broad Look
If what the cat is doing is of interest, don't move in too close, or you'll crop out the surroundings. For pictures that don't need captions or explanations, keep the cat quite small in the frame, and viewers will be better able to see what's going on.

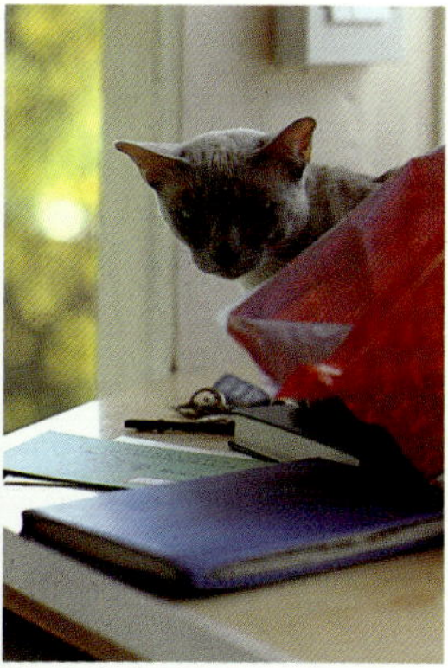

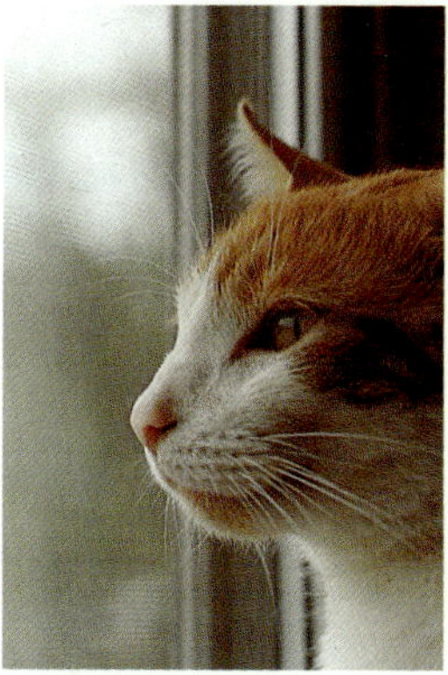

Better Composition
If the cat is doing something active, try to avoid centering it in the picture. Central subjects look static—whereas your picture will be more dynamic if you make the composition asymmetrical.

The most active compositions are those where the cat is at the intersection of two imaginary lines, each ⅓ of the way into the frame.

EXPRESSING CHARACTER

Cats are highly intelligent creatures, and each has a unique character of its own. Even identical kittens in a litter soon begin to behave differently: one may be bossy, and turn its back on the camera; while another is affectionate and curls up obediently in front of the lens. Indeed, you'd often swear your cat was human, the way it seems to smile contentedly after being fed, and struts around with an aloof frown when it doesn't get its own way. Other times the veneer of civilization wears thin, and your family cat turns into a puma, all claws and shining white teeth.

Catching a cat's personality on film is a challenge to any photographer—by comparison, making an attractive likeness seems easy. To reveal character you must first be completely confident with your camera, so that you can react to your cat's expressions and activities without the delay of fumbling with unfamiliar controls; second, you need to know your cat well enough to anticipate how it will react in every situation; and finally, you need quick reactions to catch the fleeting but revealing grimaces and gestures.

These aren't impossible demands—after all, if your cat has allowed you to share its home for a year or more, you probably know each other's habits quite well by now! The other two skills improve with practice, of course. In the next few pages we take a look at the different aspects of a cat's character, and show you how you can try to emphasize each in your photos. If you succeed, you'll be rewarded with an outstanding picture in which your cat really comes to life, and looks as if it's about to spring from the frame into the viewer's lap.

A Happy Cat

Cats have an uncanny knack of beating you to the most comfortable chair! This time, though, the cat's owner swallowed her pride and snapped the tabby's smug grin.

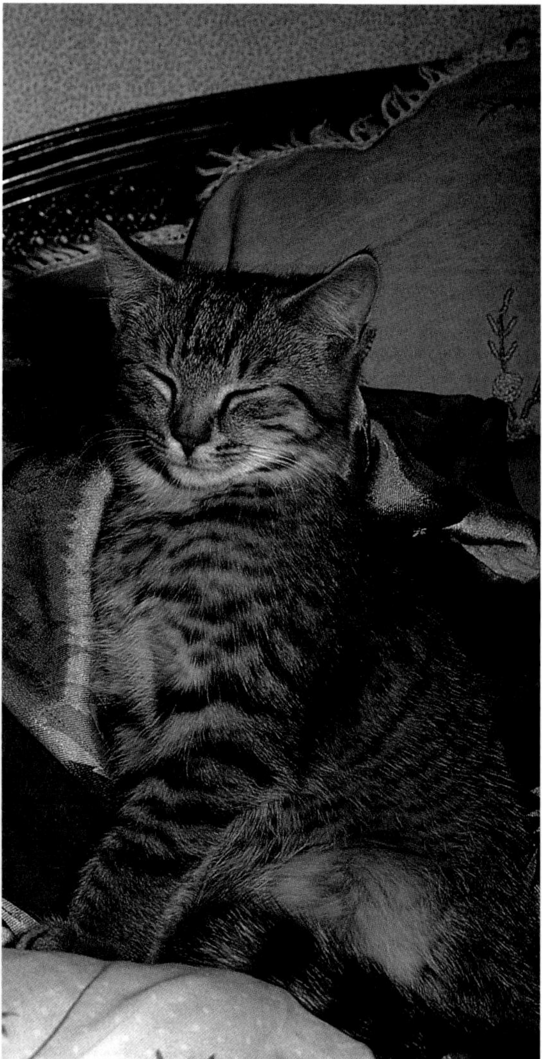

FELINE EXPRESSIONS

"Smile please" . . . "Watch the birdy" . . . "Look a little more serious" . . . these phrases are the stock-in-trade of the portrait photographer. Your cat, of course, will ignore them all. Unlike human expressions and gestures, a cat's actions and the appearance of its face and body are dictated not by choice and mood, but by reflex action and conditioning. A hungry cat doesn't sit and think to itself "If I walk over to my owner, meow and rub against his legs, perhaps he'll feed me." When your cat pesters you for food, it's going through a complex ritual that is part inherited, part learned from its mother, and part taught by you.

What has this insight into feline behavior got to do with photography? A surprising amount. If your cat's face momentarily assumes a particularly appealing expression, it is useful to know that conditioning—not whim—put it there. To reproduce the same expression, or a whole range of bodily gestures that a cat makes in response to what it senses, all you need to do is to reproduce the stimuli that were there initially.

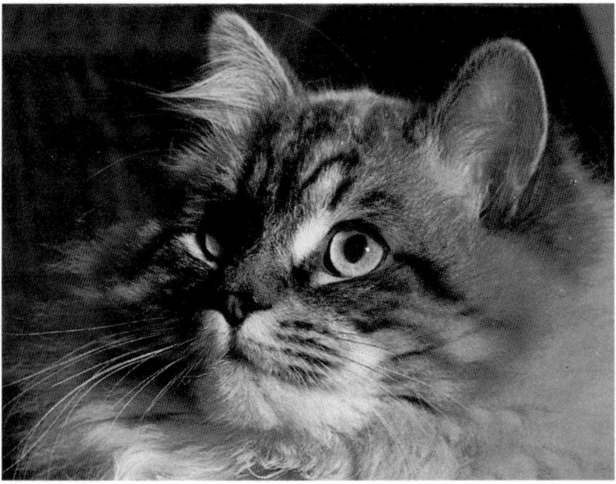

Feline Responses

Hunger and anger are obvious examples of primal instincts that provoke a particularly strong and visible response, but there are other ways to get your cat to display characteristic expressions and postures. Think about each of the cat's signals in turn.

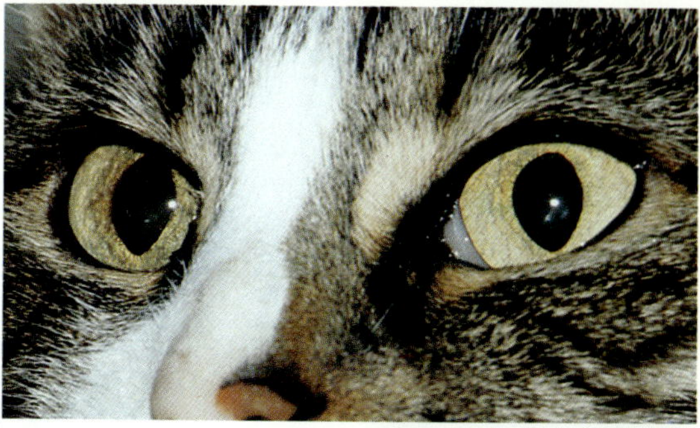

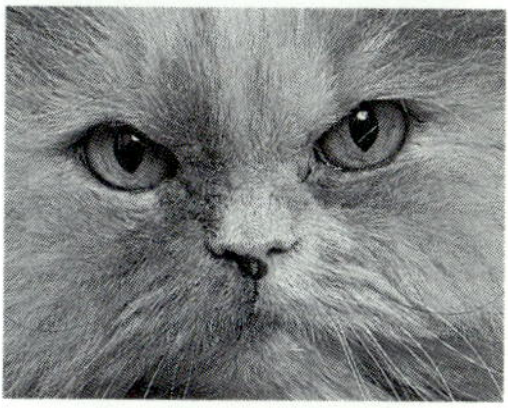

Eyes

When a cat is happy, its eyes are almost closed with pleasure, and a picture that shows such an expression instantly conveys happiness and placidity. You probably know of ways to make your cat happy, but the simplest is just to stroke it before taking the picture.

Wide eyes suggest alertness, and you can produce this expression with the promise of food. The picture will look dead though, if there is no highlight in the cat's eyes, as is likely in dull weather outdoors. Put the highlight back using fill-in flash outdoors (see page 55) and with a table lamp indoors.

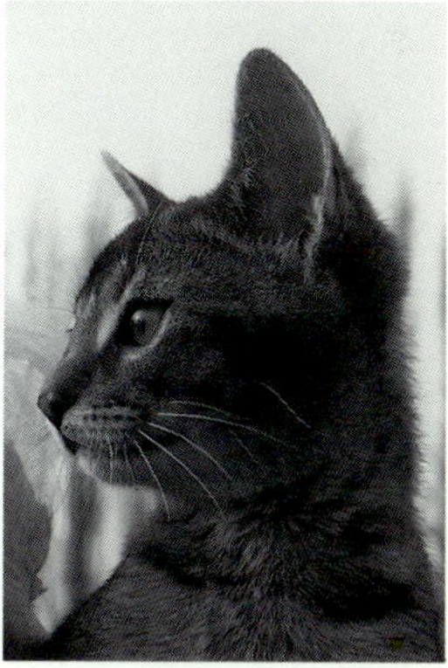

Ears

Cats have very sensitive hearing, and remarkably maneuverable ears. Many of a cat's most amusing expressions are the result of it swivelling one ear to eavesdrop on a sound coming from behind. To reproduce the characteristic pricked-up ears expression, get someone behind the cat to make a scratching sound. Be ready with the shutter release, though, because if the cat thinks the noise merits attention, it will turn its whole head after this one ear check.

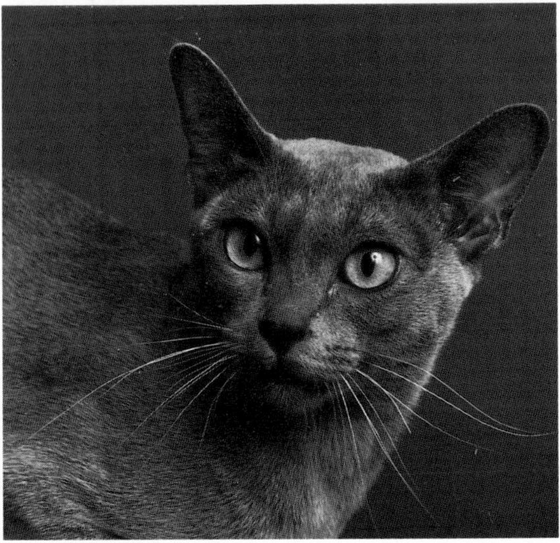

Nose and Whiskers
These share the same muscles and react together. If you're concentrating on the cat's face, you can evoke a very cute expression by gently touching the whisker tips. The cat will crinkle its nose, and the whiskers will point forward. Remember to close the aperture down, to keep the cat's eyes sharp.

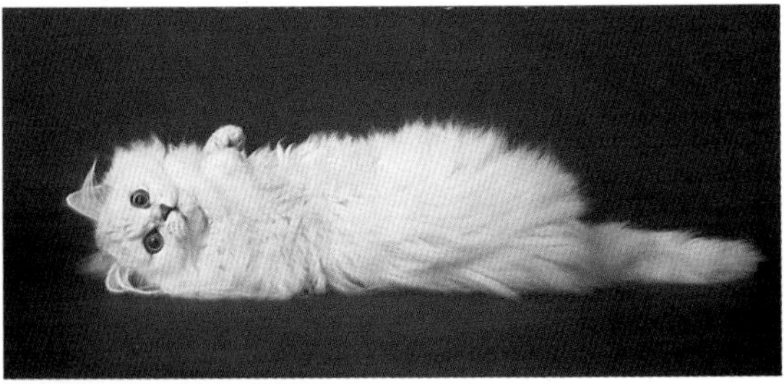

Fur
A cat will puff out its fur when it meets another cat, or when it is preparing to fight. Nobody would want to make an adult cat do this for the camera, but kittens often play at fighting, and will do a passable imitation of pop's threat display given the time and another kitten to impress.

Mouth

Cats' mouths are not particularly expressive—except in anger, when the lips go back. However, a cat will sometimes curl its lips in a grin when it detects an interesting smell. Unfortunately, what smells good to a cat often repels its owner, and only experiment will reveal what makes your cat smile. First try old socks!

Tail

Cats' tails are very expressive. Use a slow shutter speed to blur the wagging of a tail prior to a leap. Tails are used for balance, too—and a picture that shows a cat with its tail bolt upright will generally suggest concentration. Put the cat on a narrow rail such as a fence-top to straighten out the tail.

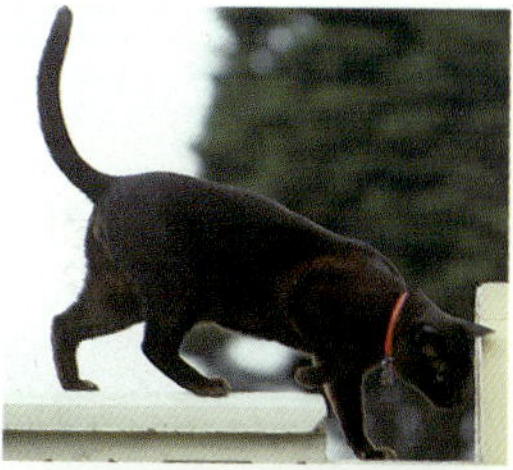

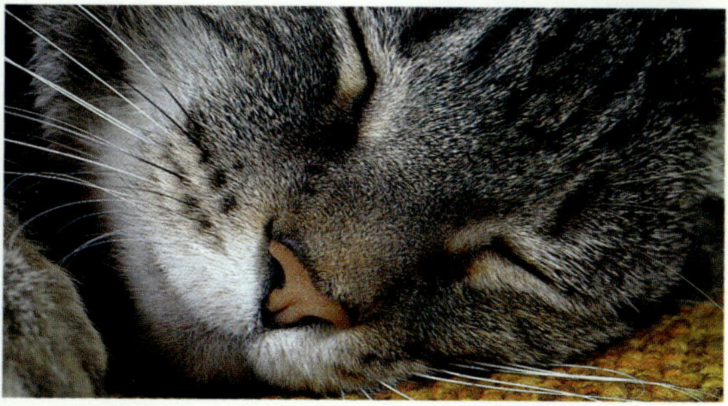

Telling Details

There's no special reason why your picture should show all of the cat: sometimes you'll find that a detail is more expressive than a full-scale portrait. Perhaps you've watched your cat walking along behind a piece of furniture, with only its tail showing? Think how much the swishing of that tail says—you can almost chart the cat's progress by the shapes it makes.

You could make a "tailpiece" for your cat album using a series of pictures on this theme, but the cat's other expressive signals highlighted here make qually good subjects for detail pictures. Close in using the equipment described on page 23, or by enlarging your existing photographs and trimming off the unwanted edges.

When taking very close pictures such as this, you'll get best results if you set a small aperture such as $f/11$.

CATCHING ACTION

A healthy cat is an active creature, always on the go. The camera gives you the option of portraying your cat's swift movements in a variety of ways: freezing action in mid-leap; blurring it for an evocative suggestion of swift motion; or a mixing of techniques that combines both sharpness and flowing lines.

Successful action photography primarily requires fast reflexes on the part of the person behind the camera, but the correct equipment certainly helps. A motor-drive or autowinder allows you to take sequences of pictures in quick succession. Set for continuous exposure, though motor-drives use a lot of film, so you may prefer to use this accessory simply in one-shot mode: here the film is advanced only when you take your finger from the shutter release, and film is consumed more sparingly. KODAK DISC Cameras and some 35 mm cameras have built-in film winders. But for most SLR cameras, autowinders and motor-drives are accessories. Finally, for some special action techniques you will need an electronic flash unit. Make sure that this is of the automatic type (often called "computer flash") which gives a burst of light of very short duration.

How Fast?

What is the slowest shutter speed that will arrest your cat's movements? Well, it depends. When you are using a telephoto lens, and the cat is moving quickly across the frame close to the camera, then only the fastest of speeds will freeze its motion. Conversely, if you use a wide-angle lens and the cat is moving slowly towards the camera, then a much slower shutter speed will do the trick. Here is a list of minimum speeds to freeze motion when the cat's body (tail excluded) fills a quarter of the frame width. Use faster speeds when its image is bigger; you'll get away with slower ones when the cat fills less than a quarter of the frame.

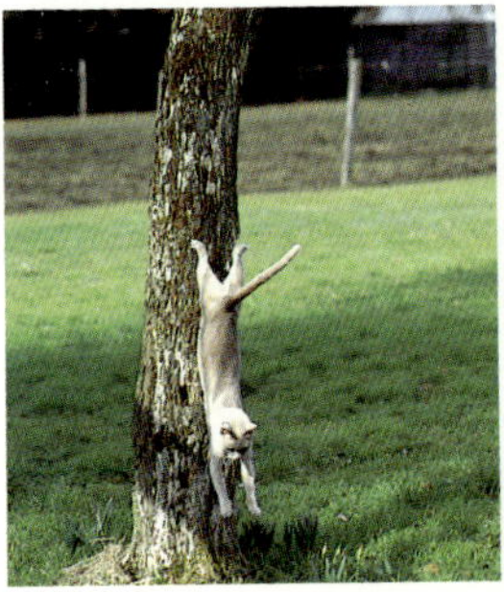

cat's action	direction of movement	
	crossing frame	towards/away from camera
Walking	1/125	1/60
Trotting	1/250	1/125
Running	1/500	1/250
Springing	1/1000	1/500
Jumping down (eg. from table)	1/2000	1/1000

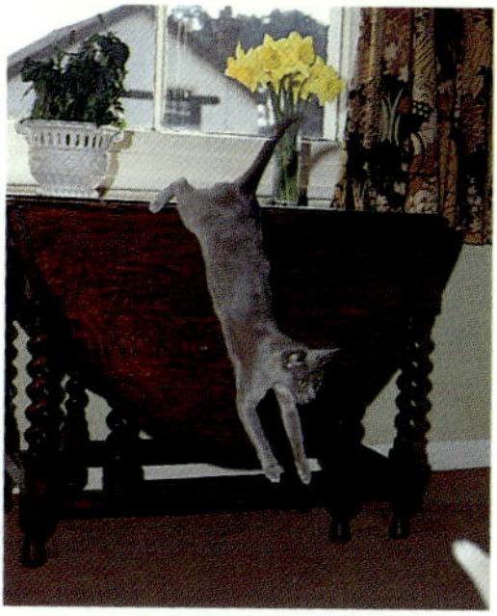

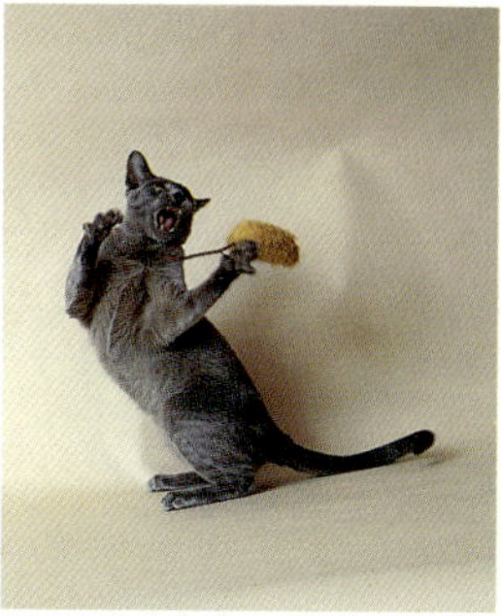

Flash to Freeze Action ▲

Most automatic flash units give a very brief pulse of light, and the duration of the pulse depends on how close the cat is to the flash. If flash and cat are close together, the burst of light may last just 1/30,000 of a second. In such a short time, the cat will move an insignificant distance, and appear absolutely sharp on film.

1 For best results, take the pictures in a fairly dark room or at night.

2 Set the flash to a moderate aperture option, and set the corresponding aperture on the lens.

3 Get the cat to perform some activity about four feet from the camera—such as jumping off a stool. Prefocus on the take-off point.

4 Estimate the cat's path and frame the picture with plenty of margin for error.

5 Use food or toys to induce the action, pressing the shutter release while the cat is in flight.

Panning the Camera ▼

If the cat is crossing the frame you can combine sharpness with evocative blur by panning the camera—that is to say, by swinging the camera round to follow the cat's movement during exposure. At a fast shutter speed, panning will record the cat sharply, but cause the background to form short horizontal streaks of color. At slow speeds (1/30 second or slower), the background becomes extremely blurred, and only parts of the cat will be sharp; its head, body and possibly its tail will be sharp, but its legs will be a whirl of activity. Panning works best when the background is darker in tone than the cat.

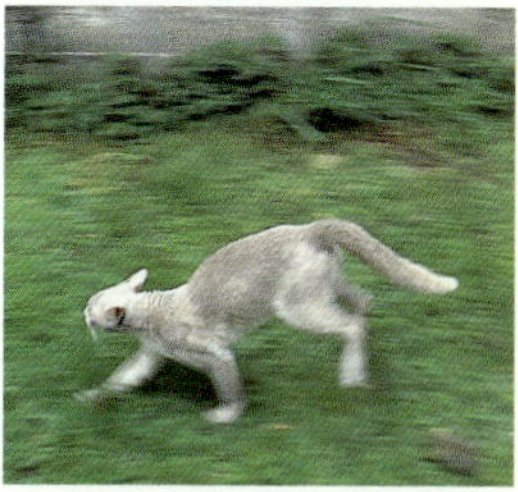

CATS AS HUNTERS

Cats are born hunters and will show amazing dexterity and speed when they track down and pounce on their prey. This activity makes for great pictures that show the cat with every muscle taut, and concentrating intently on the chase.

The cat's natural food would be birds or small rodents such as mice, voles and shrews, but only callous cat owners would want to photograph their pets in pursuit of these helpless little creatures. With a little ingenuity, though, it itsn't necessary to put the wildlife in your house or garden at peril. You can get your cat to go through the whole routine of the hunt by using suitable homemade lures—much as a trout will leap at a fly made of feathers and fur. Then you can catch the pursuit and kill on film with a clear conscience.

Making the "Prey"

Fur and feathers, in fact, make the very best lures not only for fish, but for cats too. If you have friends who hunt, you'll have no trouble obtaining scraps of either, but if you don't, or if you find the idea unappealing, buy oddments of fur or fake fur from a fabric shop. Feathers, equally, are used for decoration: try a craft shop, a milliners, or a shop that sells dried flowers, as these often also supply decorative peacock feathers. Even a feather duster can be pressed into service.

Use thread to tie the bait into a form that will convince the cat (but not the viewer of the photo), and leave a length of thread free so that you have something to pull on or swing the toy by. Gray thread is least visible on film.

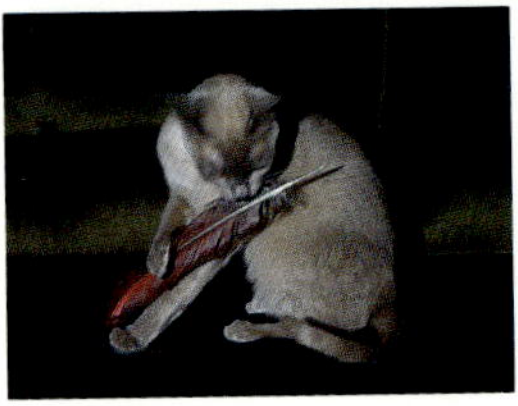

Never use fishing line, as it has a high breaking strain. If your cats gets entangled when your back is turned, it may do itself an injury in its panic to get free.

Hunting Poses

A hunting cat goes through several distinct phases, and a photographic approach that yields good pictures of one will not necessarily be best for another.

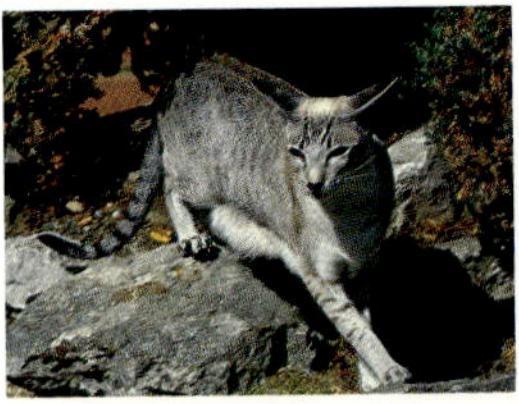

Spotting the Prey

When a cat sees a potential meal, it will freeze, and assume a very alert expression. Its ears will point forward, and be very full and erect. The eyes will be wide and bright. This pose is best portrayed in a tight close-up, since it is interesting from a facial, rather than a whole-body point of view. For a full-face picture, position the bait near the camera; for a profile, use a helper to hold the bait to one side.

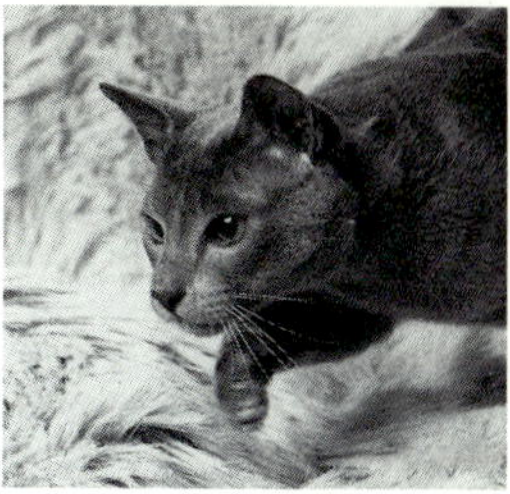

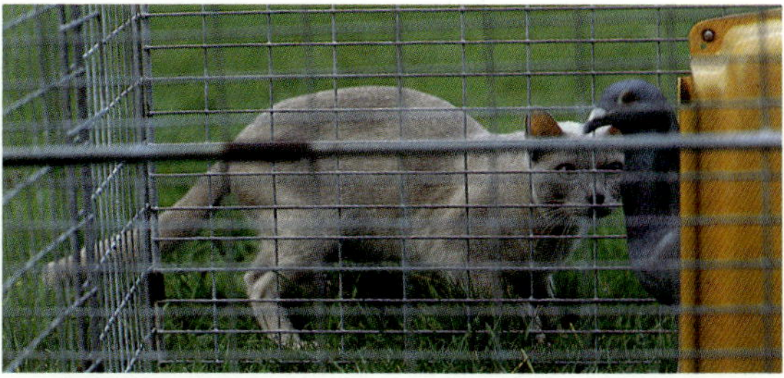

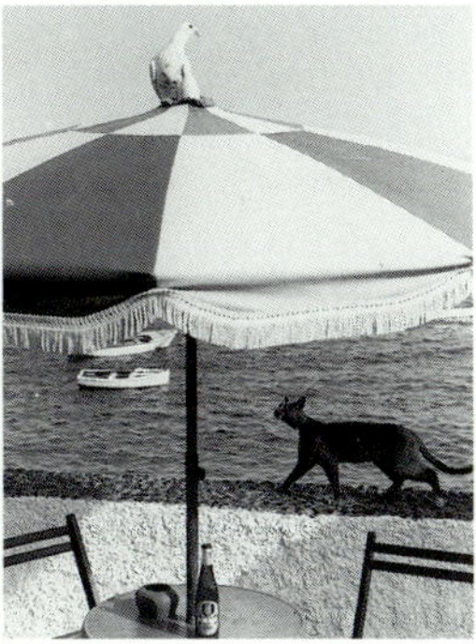

Stalking

The face of a stalking cat is equally interesting, but it is bodily postures that make good pictures at this point in the chase. Keep the camera low, and photograph the cat from the side. It will crouch as low on the ground as it can, and then worm slowly forward on its belly, with the tail held low, so as to be as inconspicuous as possible.

The gradual movements at this stage are easily photographed: there is time between advances to refocus the camera; and the gradual edging forward can be caught by the slow shutter speeds of simple cameras—whereas the kill needs a much faster shutter speed.

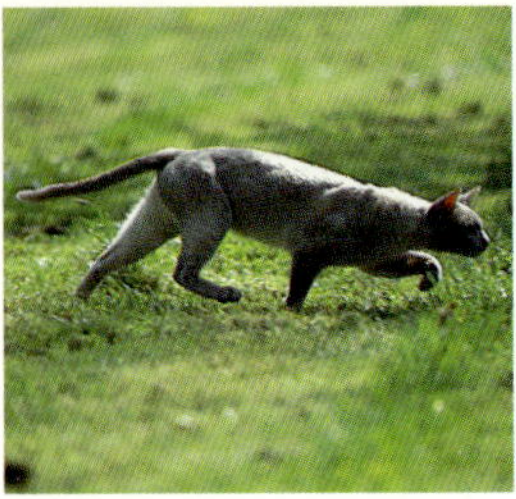

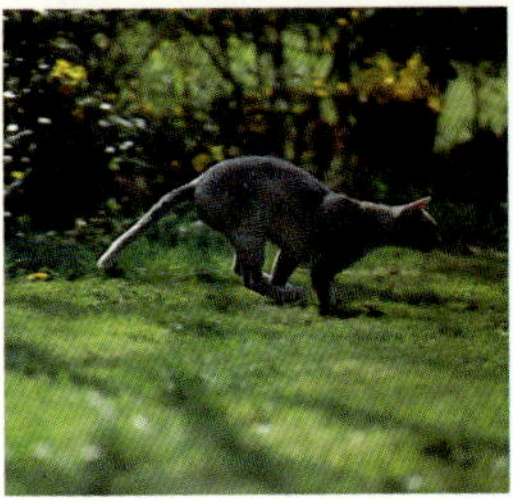

Preparing to Spring

When a cat is within striking distance of the prey, it will crouch absolutely still. This pose is very characteristic, and quite different from the stalking position. The cat's eyes will be very wide and unblinking, its whiskers forward and ears twitching, so this again makes a good full-face or profile portrait pose. The cat's tail may swish back and forth with excitement—a broader view with the camera higher up will show this most clearly.

An instant before the leap, the cat will raise and wriggle its rear-quarters slightly as it prepares to jump. This preparatory action, combined with the other signals of alertness, makes a particularly good picture.

The Spring

This looks spectacular from any angle, but is perhaps most dramatic of all when the cat is leaping towards the camera. To provoke a leap like this, hold the bait directly above the camera, and set a small aperture for maximum depth of field. Use the tips on catching action (page 90) to freeze the cat's movement.

To get some variety into pictures of your cat leaping, coax it to jump up at the prey, and down onto it, as well as just simple leaps on level ground.

Preparing To Eat

In the wild, cats will play with their catch before eating it, throwing the meal into the air with a vigorous toss of the head. Artificial baits such as fur fabric will not have a sufficiently convincing smell to provoke this behavior, but pieces of uncured fur and feather may do. You may be able to encourage this play by sprinkling the bait with a herbal extract called Valerium, which is available from herbalists and some cat supply stores.

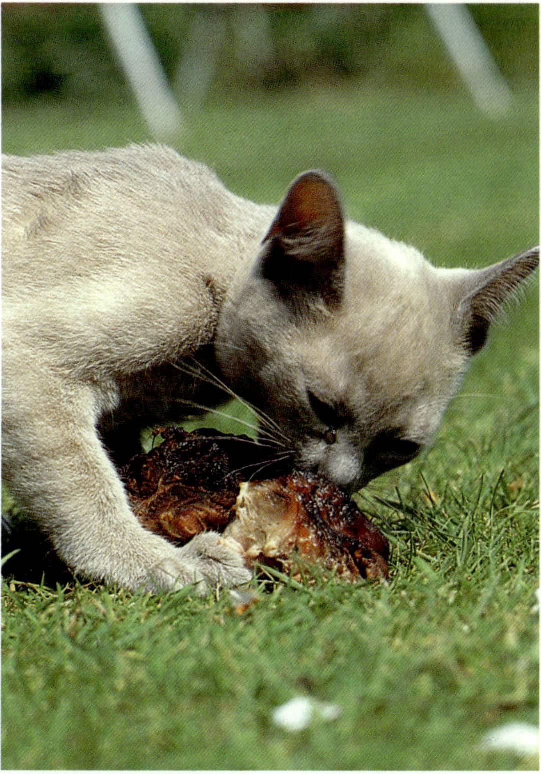

Your Cat's Wilder Side

The way cats eat canned food is very calm and sedate compared to their table manners in the wild: if your cat has free access to the yard, you're probably familiar with the spectacle of a trail of feathers and a growling cat under the bed!

This isn't a pretty sight, but if you replace the bird with a piece of raw meat or fish, you will get a glimpse of the jungle cat in your pet. Choose a low viewpoint, level with the cat's eyes if possible, and move in as close as your camera permits. The cat will probably try to run off with the food, growling all the time, so either make sure that there are no dark corners where it can hide from the camera to devour its meal, or else tie the lump of flesh down so that it cannot be dragged away.

CURIOSITY

Cats are probably the most curious of all creatures: they want to check out anything and everything. This desire to learn more about the world is charming and picturesque, and well worth recording with your camera. However, unlike other feline instincts such as the drive to hunt, curiosity is not expressed in obvious physical ways, and is therefore less easy to record on film. The simple tricks that follow will help you get pictures of your kitty satisfying its quest for knowledge.

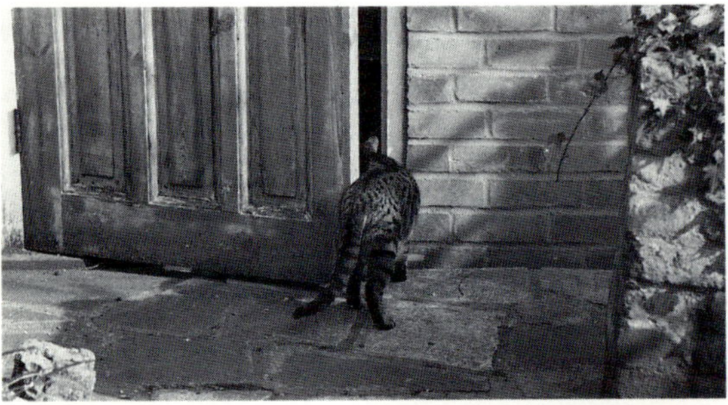

Shut Doors and Windows

No cat likes to be left out of anything—and most are convinced that there's a conspiracy behind every door. A cat soon learns which cupboard contains its food, and that the refrigerator could house something more interesting.

For pictures that show a cat's curiosity in action, station yourself and your camera on the far side of a door that opens away from you, and put the cat in the room the door leads into. Leave the door slightly ajar, and before long a nose and eye will appear, quickly followed by a paw as the cat tries to open the door. Keep the camera at floor level for the best pictures from this position,

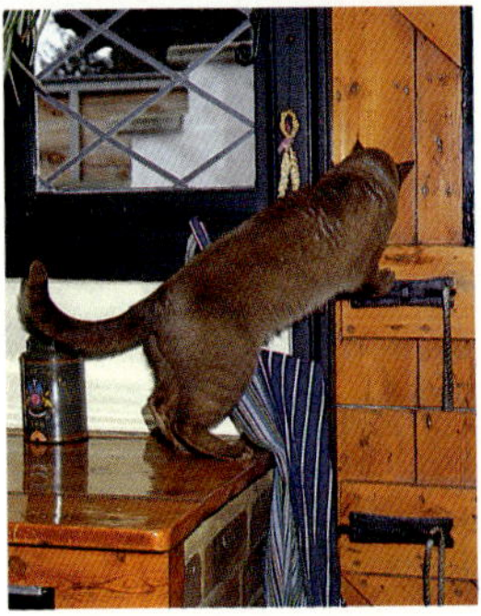

but look down on the cat from above when it's trying to escape from the room you're in—otherwise you'll just see tail and haunches.

The more ingenious breeds of cat, such as Siamese, often

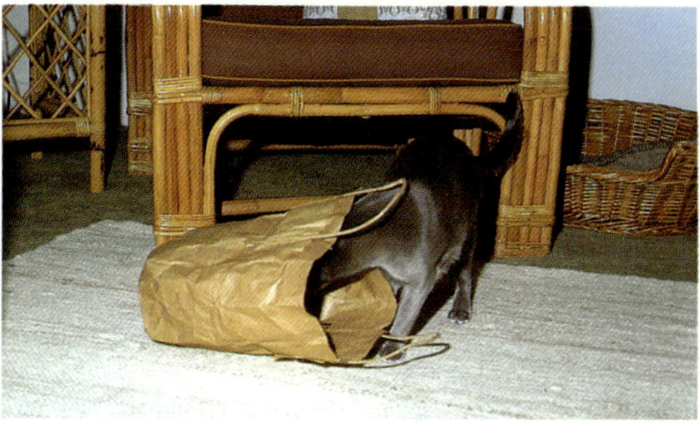

develop the ability to open the latches on doors. To get a picture of a cat doing this demands patience, but you can provide some encouragement by letting the cat see you put its dinner inside.

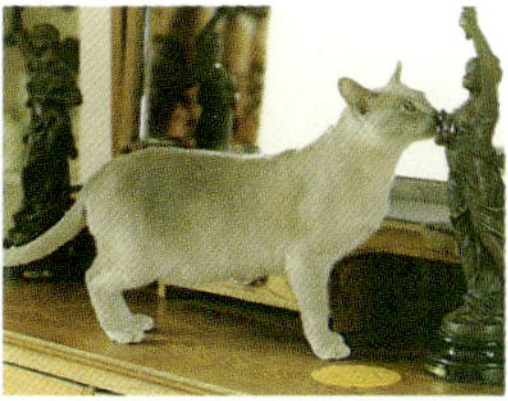

Windows initially provoke curiosity, then impatience if the cat cannot get in. Set the camera up inside for a view of a plaintive little face outside.

To a cat, a bag or a box is an open invitation—who knows what tasty morsel might be inside. Kittens cannot resist cardboard tubes, and once inside can move only forwards. Prefocus the camera on the exit end, and just wait until the kitten emerges, with a look of astonishment on its face.

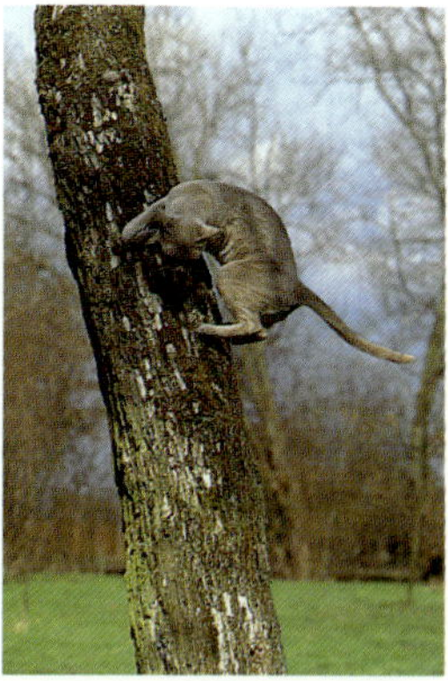

The Challenge of a Tree
Cats climb trees for safety, but out of curiosity, too. All too often the easy climb up becomes an impossible climb down, and the cat gets stuck. From ground level, the rescue looks confused—try instead to take pictures from an upstairs window with a telephoto lens.

FEELINE RITUALS

If you've watched your cat off on its own, you'll probably have glimpsed a few of the rites and rituals that occupy its time. Most of these primitive activities carried out by your pet have no real function in a modern-day domestic environment; but precisely because they are a throwback to the days when cats had to fight to survive, they can be as fascinating to document with a camera as the behavior of much more savage animals on a TV wildlife film.

Territorial Rights

Cats have a strong sense of property and have firm ideas as to how far their area extends. A cat's territory may not coincide with the boundaries of your own yard: the cat may rule a greater or lesser area. You may have seen your cat rubbing itself against trees, fences and posts, and even against your legs. This is not to scratch an itch, but to leave a scent indicating that the area is occupied. If you want to photograph your cat "autographing" the neighborhood fence posts, be prepared for a bit of stalking, and take a telephoto lens if you have one: you'll need to keep your distance, as the cat will probably come running if it spots you.

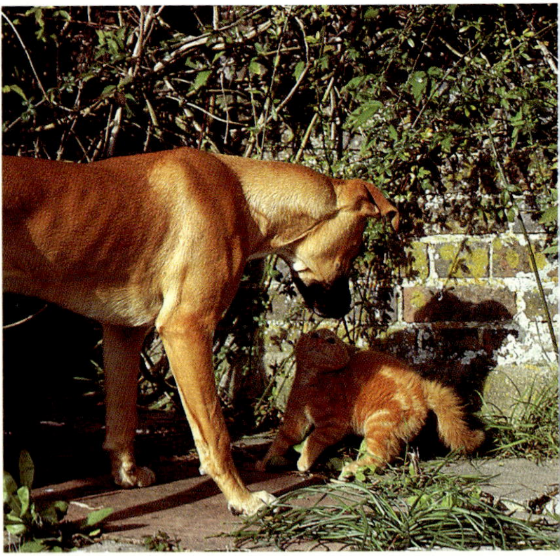

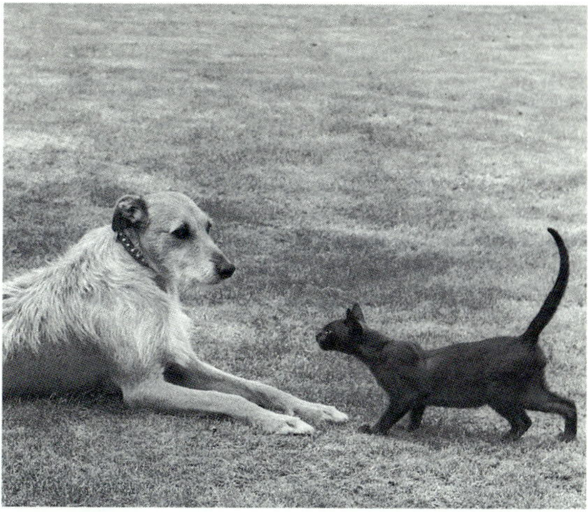

Hackles Rising
A cat's puffed-up fur when threatened is an attempt to look bigger in its adversary's eyes.

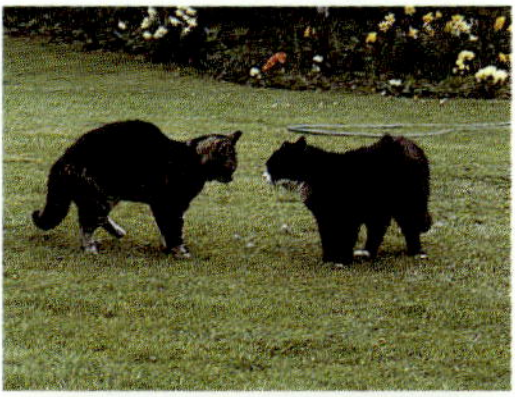

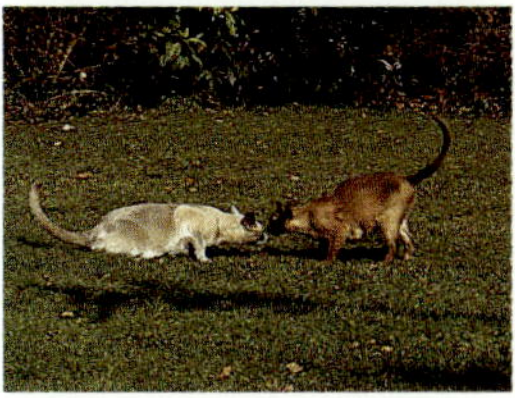

Brief Encounter
More spectacular than simple territorial marking is the stylized pantomime that takes place when two cats meet. There's always a great deal of bravado, and you'll have the chance to photograph an aspect of your cat's character seldom seen. The two cats will circle each other, sniffing, with their backs arched, the hackles lifted—puffed up like this, a cat looks larger than life. Getting a picture of this performance again means keeping well away, and using a long lens—again, pick a low viewpoint for the most spectacular view. Be quick, though, as fur will fly if one party takes offense at the other.

CATS AT PLAY

The cat is a sensible, almost serious creature, and however crazy its actions may appear, you can be sure that everything it does serves some important feline purpose. Nevertheless, much of what a cat does when it isn't eating, sleeping or washing falls into the category that humans would describe as play. It's hard to hide a smile as a kitten totters off the back of the chair that it's trying to negotiate on spindly, uncertain legs; or ends a headlong dash down the hall in a flurry of limbs, on spotting its reflection in the mirror. All these blunders make lively, humorous photographs, but you can take a lighthearted look at your playful cat in other ways, too.

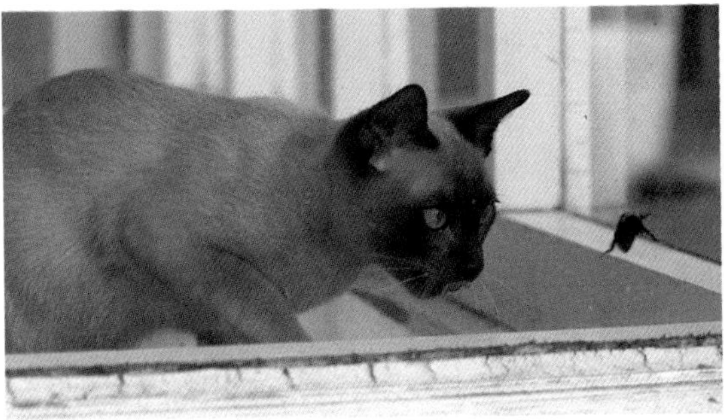

Seasonal Games

Different seasons provide changing entertainments for your cat—and varying subjects for your camera. **Summer** brings insects by the million, and you'll be able to get lively pictures of your cat in hot pursuit, as shown above. Insects on the window make it easy for the photographer—you can just focus on the glass, and wait for the cat to pounce. For a more abstract image, photograph your cat at play through the screen—you'll get a picture both of the cat itself, and of its shadow on the mesh.

Kittens are fascinated by butterflies, and will stalk them for hours, but rarely catch one. Try framing your pictures with the colorful insect in the foreground, and the kitten behind, crouched and ready to spring.

Fall brings crisp leaves, blowing in the wind. The sudden movements of a wind-borne leaf will fool a kitten into thinking that it has discovered a new animal to chase, but cats soon learn to ignore these lifeless things, so take pictures of your cat chasing leaves before it grows too wise and dignified to be taken in.

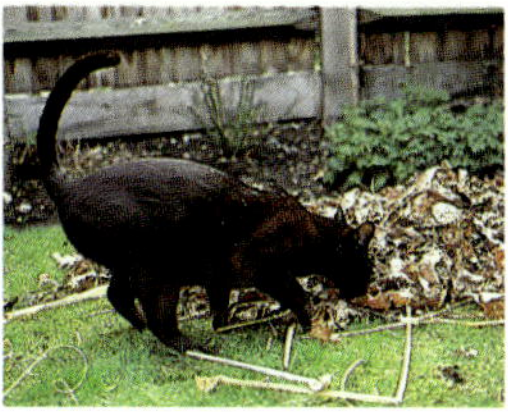

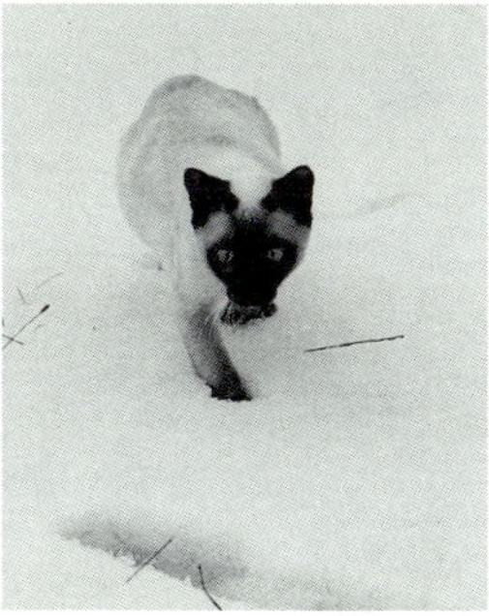

Adult cats may play in fallen leaves, but they are likely to be chasing the real animals that inhabit the debris. If you have a brown or tabby cat, you'll be able to get very attractive pictures of it playing in leaves—the russets and browns of the background set off the coloring of its coat.

Winter, too, brings new games for youngsters, but just shrugs of discomfort from adult cats. If you have a kitten when the first snow falls, keep it locked indoors until you have your camera ready. Then take the kitten outside, and snap its fascination with the falling snowflakes, and puzzlement at the overnight disappearance of familiar terrain and smells.

Spring provides less to entertain a cat than most other times of the year, but if you are alert, you may be able to get pictures of your cat on its daily tour of the yard, smelling each new flower that pushes through the soil. Keep your camera handy indoors during the spring rains, too, because a cat will often sit staring from the window as the drops splash against the pane.

Playing Together

The cat is not a pack animal, and hunts alone. Playing is often a rehearsal for the hunt, so this too is generally a solitary activity. However, you'll often get very funny pictures when there are two cats playing together.

Adults cats of the livelier breeds are not averse to a rough-and-tumble, and all kittens will play like this. They will chase each other round the room at great speed, but you'll get the best pictures when one finally catches the other, and they roll on the floor like wrestlers. Try moving in close and setting a slow shutter sped to blur their games in a whirl of fur.

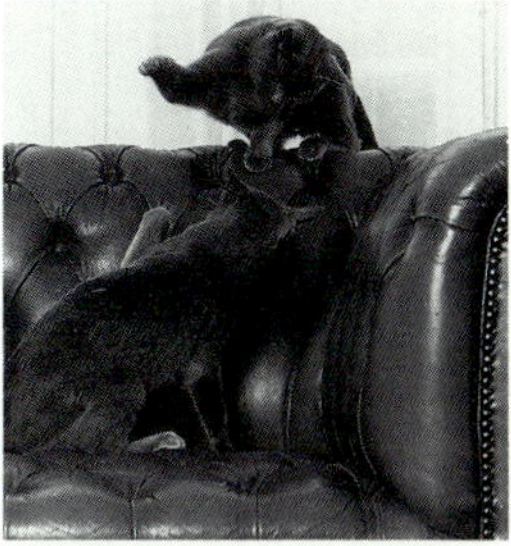

CATS AND PEOPLE

Cats form lasting bonds with their owners—and people are often as attached to their cats as they are to their human friends. It is therefore perfectly natural to photograph cats and people together, and you may as a result get a better picture of both your subjects. A frisky, uncooperative cat often calms down when sitting in the warm lap of its owner; and someone who is nervous in front of the camera will visibly relax when there is a purring pet to stroke.

If you have only a simple camera, photographing your cat with people relieves the persistent problem of getting close enough to fill the frame. Double portraits like this have two centers of interest, and can be composed with the twin subjects well within the focusing and flash range of the camera.

Some cats are so friendly that they won't even allow you the option of photographing them alone. As soon as a human figure appears, whether friend or stranger, the cat will run to them, rubbing its furry body against their legs as a token of friendship and affection. Unless you want pictures of this cat putting a nice shine on your shoes, you'll have to find another human subject to pose with your feline one!

Getting Settled
The simplest and most natural of poses show the person sitting down. Cats need no encouragement to jump into a waiting lap, and will soon curl up comfortably. A good viewpoint is quite high up, looking down on the pair—this is a particularly effective way to isolate the sitters from a cluttered domestic environment.

If you choose a lower viewpoint, make sure the person you are photographing tucks their legs under the chair, or their feet may look disproportionately large.

Sitting in someone's lap has a soporific effect on a cat, especially if it is warm and being stroked. To get the cat to look up with a more alert expression, use noise and movement.

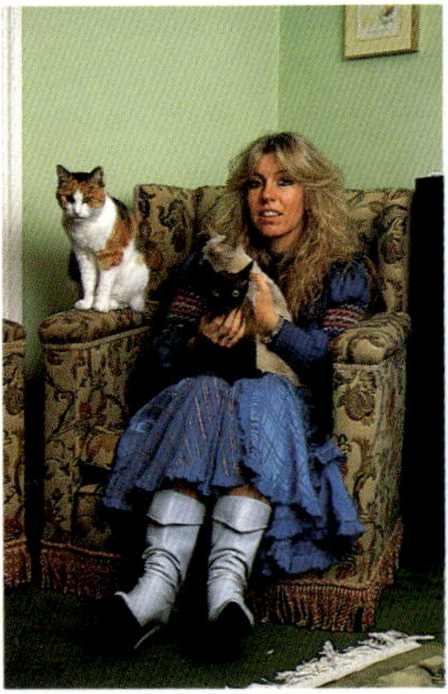

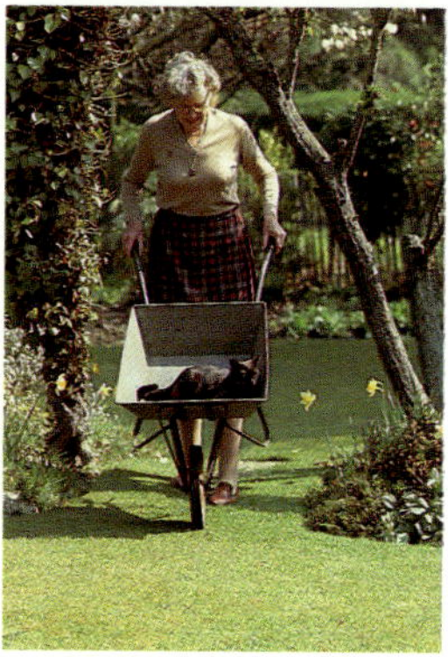

Lighting

The lighting requirements for people and cats are a little different, particularly if the cat is much darker or lighter than the skin of your human sitter. Dark fur absorbs a lot of light, and if you are photographing a dark-haired cat with a pale-skinned person, the human subject will be perfectly exposed, and the cat will be a formless blob with two glistening eyes. The solution to this problem is always to position the fairer subject farthest from the light source.

If you are using flash and can remove it from your camera's accessory shoe, take the unit well round to one side of the subjects, as explained on page 58. Then put the darkest of the pair on the side closest to the flash. If the flash is built-in, keep a dark cat close to the middle of the picture, where the flash light is at its brightest, and a light cat away from the center.

In window light, position the lighter subject farthest from the window.

Standing Poses

With arms folded, cradling the cat, the human figure makes quite a compact shape, and the two faces are quite close together. Move in to crop the picture as tightly as possible for extra drama, but with non-SLR cameras, be careful about framing, and use the close-up framing marks in your camera's viewfinder. If you have an SLR camera, you'll find that longer lenses produce more pleasing views—set a zoom lens to 100 mm.

From a position cradled in the arms, a cat will often climb up to curl round the subject's neck. The motive is usually to get a better view of the surroundings, so the cat will look wide-eyed and lively. Its muscles will also be firm and tense as it strains to keep its balance. This will show off the shape of short-haired breeds, and can be made more emphatic still by getting the person you are photographing to take a couple of paces: the cat will adjust its weight as it hangs on with its claws.

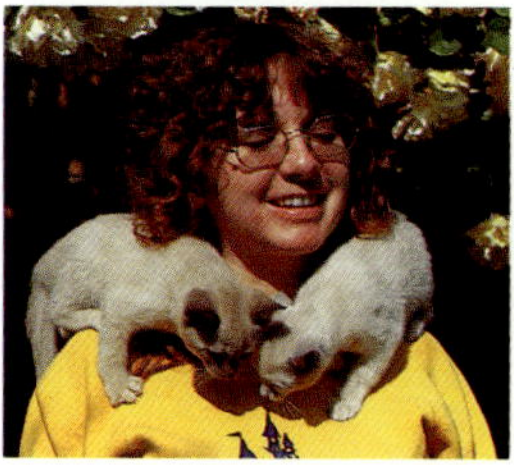

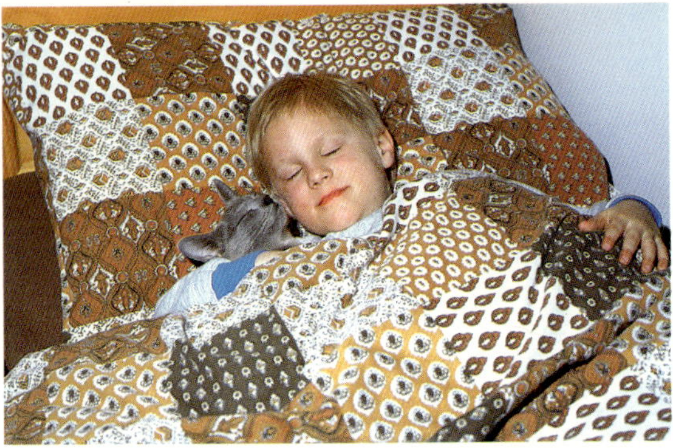

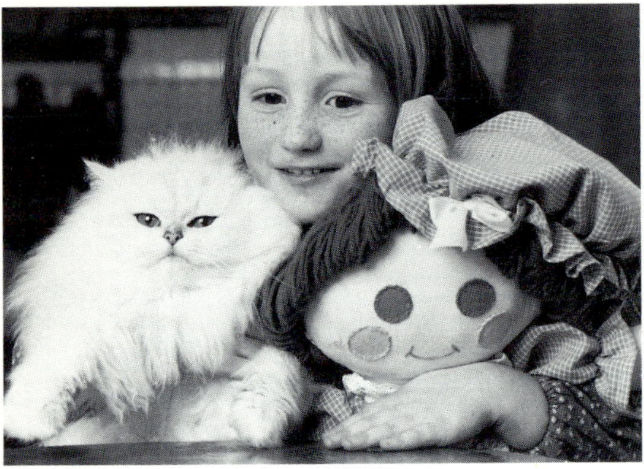

Kids and Cats

Cats and children make ideal companions, and give the photographer the opportunity of catching candid shots as they enjoy each other's company.

A word of warning—children can be unintentionally cruel, and you should keep an eye on your subjects as they play. A cat that's hurt will lash out, leaving a nasty scratch or bite. Kittens present different problems. They are defenseless, and can easily be injured by clumsy hands, even tiny ones.

Above the age of about three, though, children will be naturally gentle with a small furry creature, showing delight and pleasure at everything it does. Toys that amuse a child will often have the same effect on the cat—especially toys that move, or are shiny.

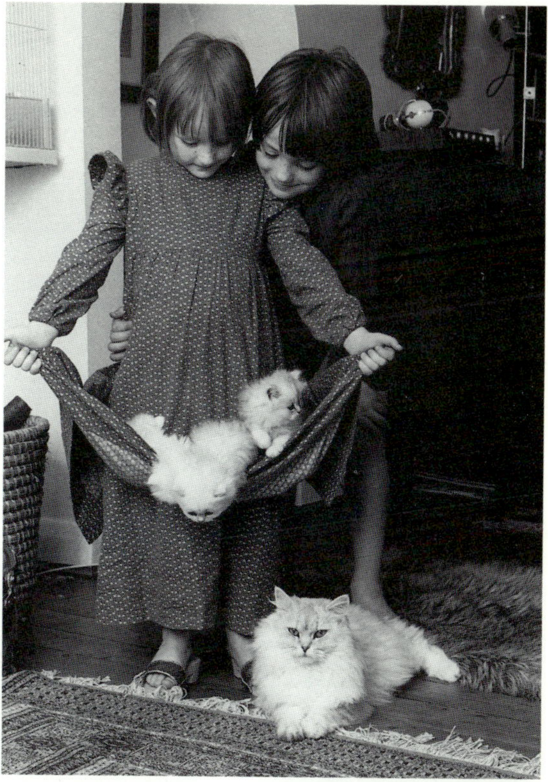

When photographing cats and children together, aim for a natural, unposed look. This is easiest if neither subject knows you are taking the picture, or when they are bored with the camera. Start by using a telephoto lens—perhaps in the garden. If the pair notice you and start acting up for the camera, keep taking pictures until they lose interest. Then move closer in.

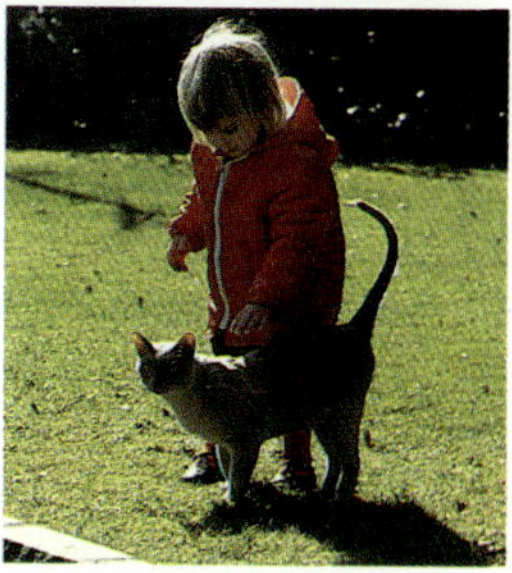

PICTURING SHOW CATS

If you are interested in cat breeding, or have been to a cat show, you'll know that pictures of pedigree cats are rather special. They not only have to display the cat to the very best advantage but they must also emphasize the particular points that breeders look for. For example, Siamese cats should appear very long and elegant; they must have a straight, whip-like tail, a long nose, and a fine bone structure. The head should look almost triangular in shape, with the ears making a straight line across the brow.

These considerations won't worry you if you just want a picture for the family album, but if you plan to breed your cat, and want the picture published in an advertisement or show catalogue, details are important. You can get information about standards of excellence for each breed from one of the governing bodies, such as the Cat Fanciers Association. These organizations draw up a "Standard of Points" for each breed: a bit like a checklist setting out the correct appearance for a particular variety of cat.

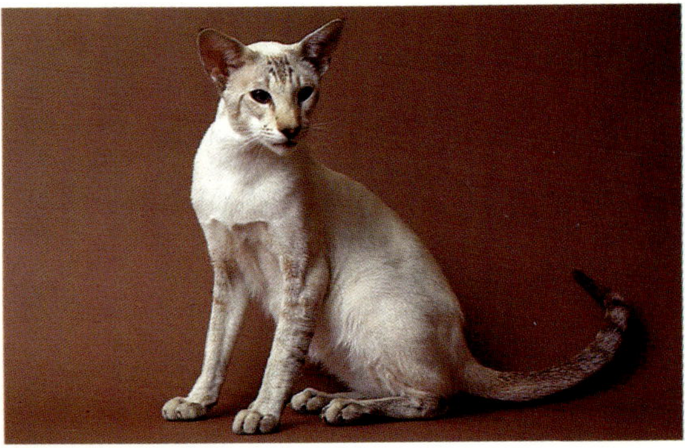

Posing the Cat

There are no set rules as to pose, but a good general guide is to take two pictures: one from the side, to show the body shape, and one looking straight at the cat from the front, including the legs.

If the cat is not your own and you are not familiar with the breed, ask the owner what needs emphasizing, and whether the cat has any weak points that should be minimized in the photograph.

Eyes and Coat

The color of a cat's coat and eyes are very important to breeders, and it is easy to make the colors appear too warm or cool in hue by selecting an inappropriate background color. Cats with pale coats will tend to pick up the color of the background most easily, so it is usually safer to photograph these cats on a neutral color such as black, white or gray, or else on a pale pastel hue. Eye color, too, can be changed by intense primary hues.

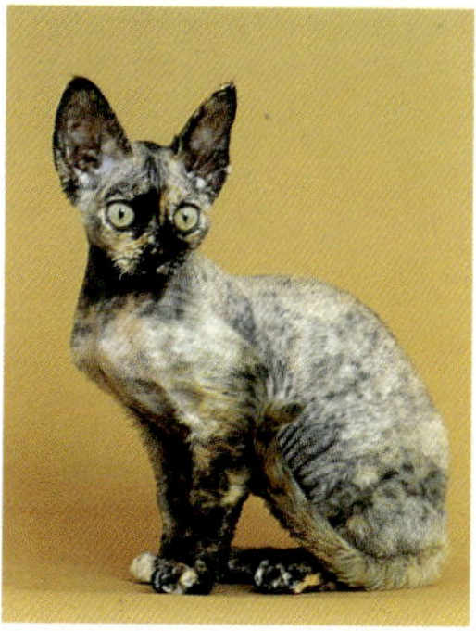

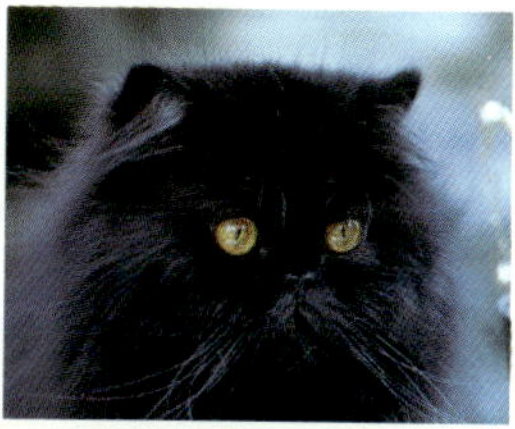

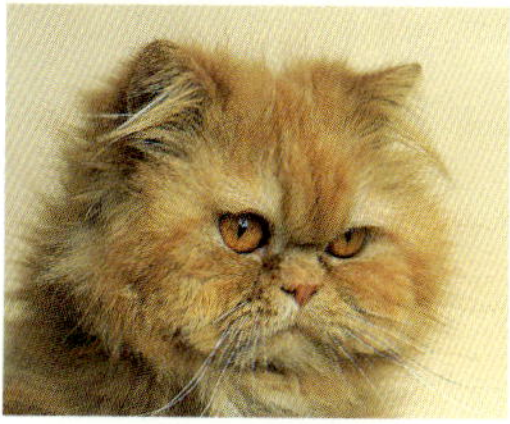

Breed Characteristics ▼

Certain breeds have unusual habits which your picture should reflect. This is a rag-doll "flopping".

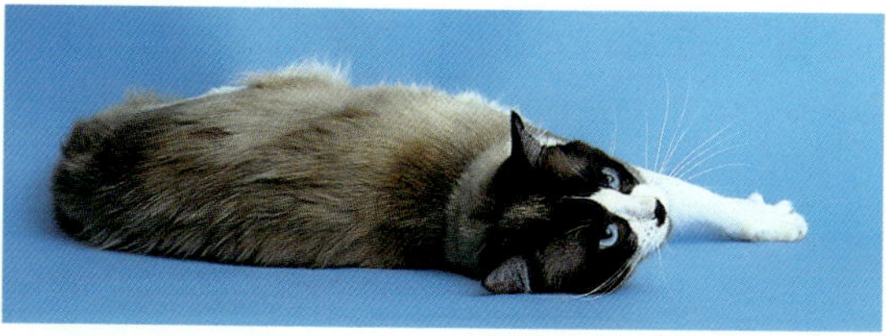

Which Film?

If the pictures are to be printed in a magazine or brochure, don't use color negative film. Instead load either medium-speed black and white negative film, such as KODAK PLUS-X Film, or transparency film such as KODACHROME 64 Film. On the other hand, if the owner just wants color prints of the pictures then use color negative film such as KODACOLOR VR 100 Film. Make sure, though, that the pictures are printed by a reputable lab, and ask for a proof to check color.

Setting Up a Home Studio

For maximum control over how your cat appears on film, you may want to take a little extra trouble with lighting. Fitted into your camera's hot shoe and pointed directly at your cat, a small flash unit creates very hard, unappealing shadows. To diffuse and soften the beam for more attractive pictures, reflect the light from a white surface such as an umbrella. This absorbs a lot of light, though, so if you are to avoid setting an unacceptably wide aperture, you'll need to use quite a powerful flash unit for bounce flash pictures.

Look for one that has a guide number (measured in feet for ISO 100 film) of 110 or more. An even better choice is a small studio flash unit such as that shown at right.

Studio flash units have several major advantages: they recycle rapidly; they are designed to operate from service supply voltage instead of batteries; they can be fitted with a variety of accessories to control the light; but most important of all, they have tungsten "modelling" lights, which simulate the effect of the flash. Thus you can see how moving one light closer to or farther from the cat affects the lighting balance.

Triggering the Flash

If you have two identical flash units, you can connect both to your camera's synchronization socket using a "Y" connector. But a more reliable way to synchronize multiple flash is to use cordless slave cells. One of these plugs into the cable of a flash unit, and closes the synchronization circuit when another flash is operated.

Measuring Flash Exposure

Unlike automatic flash units, studio flash does not adjust its output to compensate for subject distance. To set exposure you must therefore measure the combined output of all the flash units, using a flash meter. When you trigger a test flash, the meter measures the brightness, and a digital readout indicates the aperture to set.

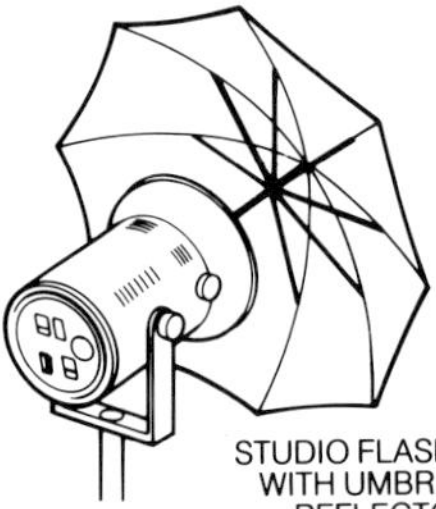

STUDIO FLASH UNIT WITH UMBRELLA REFLECTOR

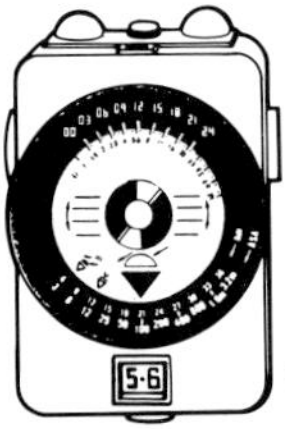

FLASH METER

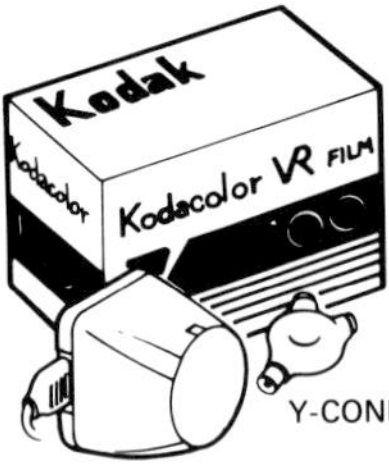

Y-CONNECTOR

SLAVE CELL

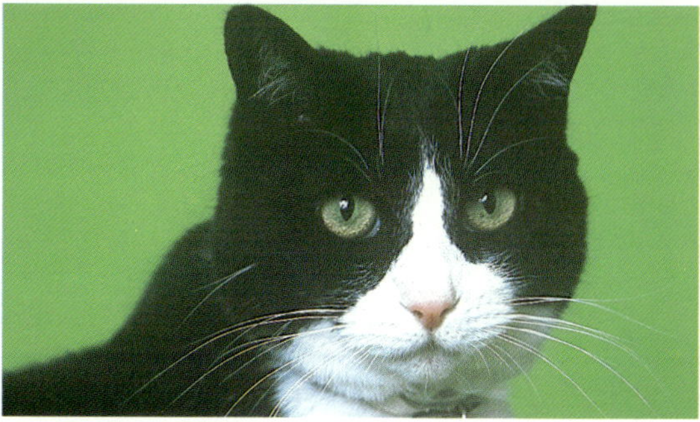

Basic Lighting Set-Ups
These three diagrams show basic ways of lighting your cat, using one, two and three light sources.

One Light with Reflector
This simplest of all studio lighting arrangements give good results at minimal expense. Start with the umbrella and reflector as shown, then experiment by moving them around to vary the depth and position of shadows.

Two Lights
With two lights, always make sure that one dominates: the second should be much less powerful or farther away, and serve only to illuminate the shadows. If the two lamps are equal in intensity, you'll create unnatural-looking double shadows.

Adding Backlighting
A third flash (even a small one) can be placed low behind the cat to provide some backlighting. This puts a ring of light around the cat, separating it from the background.

A Serious Stare
This portrait was lit using the simplest setup illustrated.

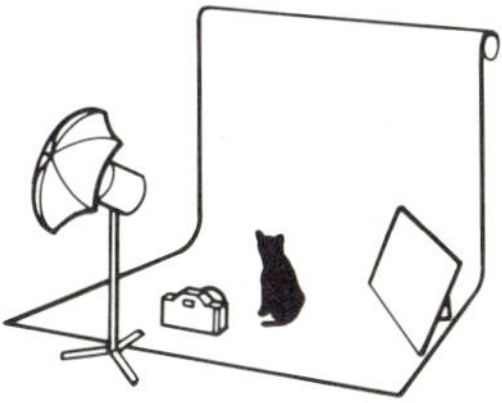

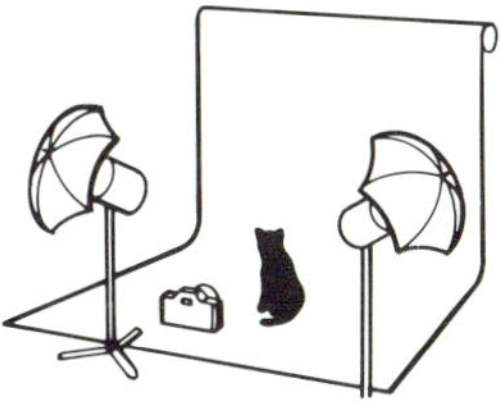

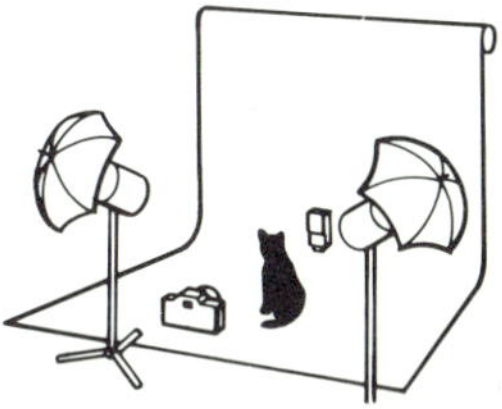

INDEX